Food
and your
Special
Needs
Child

Food
and your
Special
Needs
Child

**Antonia Chitty
& Victoria Dawson**

ROBERT HALE • LONDON

© Antonia Chitty and Victoria Dawson 2013
First published in Great Britain 2013

ISBN 978-0-7198-0790-9

Robert Hale Limited
Clerkenwell House
Clerkenwell Green
London EC1R 0HT

www.halebooks.com

A catalogue record for this book is available from the British Library

2 4 6 8 10 9 7 5 3 1

Typeset by Eurodesign
Printed in the UK by the Berforts Group

Contents

Introduction

Do you have a child with special needs or a disability? Has your child had issues with their diet? Do they have strong preferences, struggle with some foods or refuse to eat? If so, you're not alone. There are many causes of eating issues, and children with special needs are more likely to have problems.

As parents we want the best for our children, and providing nourishing meals that the family can eat together is something that we would all like. In reality, life often isn't like this. Whether your child struggles to stay at the table, isn't interested in food or has allergies, mealtimes can be a challenge. For many parents, getting food into their child to keep them healthy is a daily battle.

There are many reasons why children have problems with food. In this book you can read about both the social and behavioural issues, as well as physical causes of eating difficulties. You can learn about normal digestion and what can go wrong. This knowledge will help you to better understand what is going on when your child eats.

There is a whole chapter in this book dedicated to 'selective eating' – those children who seem to choose a very limited repertoire of safe foods. This is an enormous issue, particularly for parents of children on the autism spectrum, and we have helpful advice from experts for you to read, alongside case studies of families who explain what has worked for them.

Food can be a very emotional area, and in Chapter 5 you can look at how your child's emotions can affect their eating. Learn about managing anxiety, and eating disorders related to the emotions. There is also a chapter on allergies, food sensitivity and food intolerance.

The second half of the book, from Chapter 8 onwards, focuses on practical actions that you can take in the home and in co-operation with professionals to help everyone enjoy mealtimes again. Learn about useful tools such as food diaries and get plenty of ideas to help your child touch food, make choices, cook and grow food. These activities will all help your child improve their relationship with food and eventually expand what they eat.

There are also plenty of ideas for children with behavioural issues who struggle to stay at the table. Learn what works for other families and get expert advice on tools to engage children and make mealtimes fun. You can also read about how to move towards eating out with your child.

In addition to all this, you'll find a detailed chapter of advice on helping your child to take medication. If your child has issues with food, and special needs, the chances are that taking medication will not always be straightforward. For children who need regular medication this can be a real problem. Learn what has worked for other parents and get tips from experts.

Finally, we have rounded up all the resources that will help you support your child in Chapter 12. From larger bibs to helpful websites, Chapter 12 contains the stepping stones you need to make eating and mealtimes a happy part of family life again.

Chapter 1
How We Eat

Eating and digestion is something we take for granted, until it goes wrong. If your child struggles with food, it can be extremely difficult to cope. Mealtimes can become a battleground, and the idea of sitting down together to enjoy a family meal a distant dream. You may worry about meeting your child's nutritional needs too.

This chapter explains how a child's digestive system develops, and helps you to start to understand more about how things can go wrong.

Introduction to eating

Are mealtimes a challenge for your child? If so, you are not alone. Many families face regular battles over food, and for children with special needs or disabilities food can be a particular issue. Read about Laura and her son Callum for an insight into eating issues:

Laura's son Callum has autism spectrum disorder, learning difficulties, hypotonia and hypermobile joints. He has a limited diet; he will only eat small amount of foods, and is very specific about the temperature he will tolerate. Laura says, 'If he is anxious eating is the first thing that will go. If anyone touches his food or even comments on the fact he is eating (depending on his anxiety levels) he will stop eating.'

Callum's eating issues first appeared as a baby. Laura says, 'He had really bad reflux from around five months old. He didn't take solids until he was around fourteen months, then was seen at the outpatients' clinic from around eighteen months for weight loss and constipation. He was so constipated that every time he tried to go he would vomit.'

Now nine years old, Callum is on prescribed vitamin and calcium supplements. Laura says:

" We just live with his eating issues and try and not stress about it anymore. Leaving him till he is hungry doesn't apply, as he doesn't recognize the sensation of hunger. We accept now that he will go through phases where his eating is slightly better, and others, particularly when he is stressed or out of his routine, when the eating goes and we just need to focus on getting calories into him for energy. "

Eating at school has been a particular issue for Callum. Laura explains:

" There are periods where he hasn't been able to cope with being in the lunch hall. For almost a year he ate in the class with a teacher, and then they slowly integrated him back into the hall, with his back to his peers. If he is anxious he just won't eat in school. School have to think carefully about who he sits with as if anyone attempts to touch his food whilst he's eating he will stop and not touch the rest of his food. He has the same packed lunch for school every day and has done since he started reception, with the exception of a Friday where he will eat school dinner if it is fish and chips. Socially it makes things difficult as a family as he will not eat in a restaurant. "

Callum's food issues have had consequences for Laura herself. She says:

" It caused me insane amounts of stress in the early days. Even now I still get anxious, as I know there are periods where his diet is really unhealthy, but it's that or he doesn't eat. I do my best to ensure his nutritional needs are met and otherwise we try and not stress about it because that only makes the whole situation worse. Other people do judge you but I've given up worrying about that as my concern is him. "

Laura has some advice for other parents in the same situation:

❝ *Try and not get too stressed about it. Sometimes you just need to relax and go with what they will eat and try and introduce new foods in a relaxed way. It's important to figure out the basis of your child's issues – rule out any physical difficulties first of all. Look at how the environment/sensory issues affect how and what your child eats. Use dietary supplements if necessary. Don't listen to well-meaning advice if it doesn't feel right – for example 'hiding food'. With many autistic children, if you hide a 'bad' food in a 'good' food, you have contaminated the good food so they won't eat that either. I wish I'd spent less time worrying about Callum's food issues. Eating issues can be very specific to individual children and it is a learning process, but it's hard to work through it if you are really worried.* ❞

What we need to eat

Children need food to help them grow healthily and resist infection. A good diet will help your child build up strength and ensure they have the energy to complete everyday tasks. The right food can help your child concentrate and learn better. In the long term, a healthy diet minimizes the chance of future health problems from dental decay to heart disease. As the parent of a child with special needs or a disability, you may know this already, and feel that it just adds to the stress you experience when feeding your child. Read on to learn more about a healthy diet for your child, and how to adapt this when eating is not as straightforward as you would like.

The food we need

The food we need to stay healthy includes:

✓ **Carbohydrates** – to give you energy. Found in potatoes, rice, cereals, pasta, bread and some fruit and vegetables. Made up of glucose and other monosaccharides
✓ **Fats** – to give you energy. Found in dairy products, red meat and some poultry and fish. Made up of glycerol and fatty acids
✓ **Proteins** – to help your body grow and repair itself. Found in meat, poultry, fish, dairy products, eggs and beans. Made up of amino acids
✓ **Vitamins and minerals** – to keep your body functioning healthily. Vitamins are found in fruit and vegetables and dairy products. Minerals are found in fruit and vegetables

People also need fibre in their diet to ensure that they can digest their food. Fibre is found in fruit and vegetables. It passes through the body and helps with the excretion of waste products.

How much?

As well as getting a mix of carbohydrates, fats, proteins, vitamins and minerals, there are also recommendations for the amount of food children need at different ages and stages. More active children will need more calories. If you are already getting advice from a dietitian, he or she may have given you guidelines that relate to your child's particular age, size and level of activity.

Recommended daily calorie intake

	Boys (kcal per day)	Girls (kcal per day)
Toddlers 1–3	1230	1165
Pre-schoolers 4–6	1715	1545
School-age children 7–10	1970	1740
Teenagers 11–14	2220	1845
Teenagers 15–18	2755	2110
Adults	2550	1910–1940

What's 'healthy'?

A healthy diet for a child isn't the same as a healthy diet for an adult. Children are growing, which means they need plenty of calories for energy, and they should have a higher proportion of fat in their diet than adults. Fat provides energy, essential fatty acids and fat-soluble vitamins. Babies and toddlers can have up to 40%–50% of their calories as fat, and children and teenagers up to 35%. Low fat, high fibre diets are not healthy for children as they do not provide enough energy.

If your child struggles with eating you may need to focus on providing high calorie nutrition-packed foods so that they get the maximum benefit from what they do consume. If you are worried that your child is overweight, don't impose a 'diet'. Build more activity into everyday life. Spend time together going for a walk, walking the dog, playing ball, etc. If you have serious concerns, seek advice from your child's GP or another relevant health care professional. You may be advised to see a dietitian who will help you devise a healthy diet for your child and incorporate more activity instead of cutting calories, which can cause problems for children who are still growing and developing.

The more active your child is, the more they need to eat. Children have small stomachs so need food that is high in energy, plus full of vitamins and minerals, particularly calcium, iron, and vitamins A and D. They need small, regular meals. Like adults, children need fibre for healthy digestion, but too much fibre can mean that a food is very filling and doesn't provide a child with enough calories. Moderate the amount of brown rice and wholemeal pasta you serve, and don't add extra bran to children's meals as this can reduce absorption of vitamins. As you can see from the table on page 13, children need to eat more calories than an adult of a comparative body size.

Although children can eat more fat, parents still need to understand what makes up a healthy diet. Children should consume full-fat milk, meat, oily fish, eggs and cheese, as well as nuts, seeds and avocados, all of which are good sources of fat. Children under two should not have semi-skimmed milk. Cakes, sweets, chocolate and crisps should be kept as an occasional treat. Food preferences are often established early in life, so moderating treats is important so children learn about a healthy diet. Keep sugary foods to a minimum and avoid offering them as snacks between mealtimes.

The eatwell plate opposite shows the proportions of each type of food that should be eaten over the course of a day by adults and children aged five plus. You may be able to achieve a balance easily, but don't despair if your child eats only very limited types of certain food groups. Understanding what foods fall into which groups can help you decide where input is needed. If your child eats no vegetables, for example, but will eat apples, start by ensuring that they have some apple every day.

Andrea's son has Asperger's syndrome. He has a limited diet and is unwilling to try any unfamiliar foods. Read on to find out more about Tom, and about how Andrea helps him eat as healthily as possible. She explains:

" *As one example, he will only eat one type of sliced brown bread; the only fruit: bananas/apples; the only vegetables: raw carrots, potatoes (he did eat peas until recently); he has exactly the same packed lunch every day: white bread cheese rolls, a buttered pancake, Wotsits or Mini Cheddars, an iced biscuit. I believe that these issues are definitely part of his ASD.* "

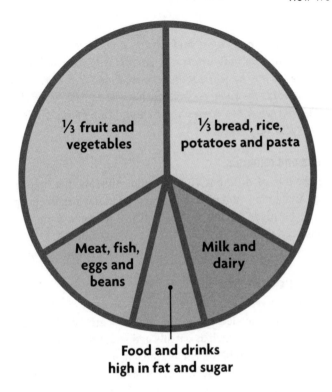

⅓ fruit and vegetables

⅓ bread, rice, potatoes and pasta

Meat, fish, eggs and beans

Milk and dairy

**Food and drinks
high in fat and sugar**

Andrea explains how she manages Tom's eating issues:

❝ *I never force the issue, as this does not work! I feel that, even though his likes are limited, he does have a balanced diet and is a very fit and healthy 8-year-old. It is more important that he enjoys his food now and has a good appetite, and then as he gets older he will hopefully accept more foods. Friends know his condition and are very understanding when we go to tea and make sure they give him what he likes.* ❞

Andrea shares her advice for other parents:

❝ *It's difficult, as I know some parents will have far more serious concerns than we have had. But I feel that the most important things are for a child to have some foods they enjoy and to have a good appetite. If you can find at least one food in each food group which they enjoy, then that is a good start. It doesn't matter that Tom only wants raw carrots with his chicken and pasta! One day he will eat them cooked. And it doesn't matter that he wants the same packed lunch every day. The good thing is that his lunch box comes home empty! Don't force the issue, unless it is very serious.* 〞

Vitamins and minerals

There are lots of different vitamins and minerals that help us stay healthy. A vitamin is something that we need to stay healthy but cannot generally be made by our bodies and has to come from our diet. Humans need thirteen vitamins: four fat-soluble ones, A, D, E, and K, and nine water-soluble vitamins (eight B vitamins and vitamin C).

WHAT VITAMINS DO

- **Fat-soluble vitamins** can be stored in the body.
- Vitamin A – needed for vision and cell growth. It is found in orange vegetables such as carrots and sweet potatoes, ripe yellow fruits, leafy vegetables such as spinach, and liver.
- Vitamin D – helps us metabolize minerals. Lack of vitamin D can cause rickets (osteomalacia). Your body can manufacture it if you get enough sunshine on the skin. In the developed world vitamin D is added to staple foods, such as milk, to avoid disease caused by deficiency
- Vitamin E – an antioxidant, which means it helps cells stay healthy. It is found, in various forms, in corn oil, soybean oil, margarine, wheat germ oil, sunflower and safflower oils, as well as avocado, asparagus, broccoli and kiwi fruit.
- Vitamin K – involved in the blood clotting process. It is found in green leafy vegetables.
- **Water-soluble vitamins** need to be consumed regularly as any extra vitamins are not stored in the body, but excreted in urine.
- B1, thiamine, is essential for our nerves to work well. It is found in yeast and grains.
- B2, riboflavin, helps us metabolize fats, carbohydrates and proteins.
- B3, niacin, is important for cardiovascular health.

- B5, pantothenic acid, is important in a range of metabolic functions.
- B6 helps us metabolize proteins and glycogen, amongst other functions.
- B7, biotin, is necessary for cell growth, the production of fatty acids, and the metabolism of fats and amino acids.
- B9, folic acid, is used to make and repair DNA, to produce healthy red blood cells and prevent anaemia. It is important for growth.
- B12, cobalamin, helps the brain and nervous system function.
- B vitamins are found in asparagus, avocados, bananas, bread, broccoli, brown rice, fortified cereal, dairy products, eggs, fish, green beans, leafy vegetables, liver, meat, mushrooms, oatmeal, pasta, peanuts, popcorn, pork, potatoes and tree nuts.
- Vitamin C is part of the process for making collagen and healing wounds. It is also an antioxidant and a natural antihistamine. It is present in fruit and vegetables.
- Most children don't need vitamin supplements. If you are concerned that your child isn't getting enough vitamins, talk to your health visitor or GP. They may decide that you will benefit from a visit to a dietitian. If your child has a very limited diet the paediatrician, GP or other health professional may prescribe supplements.

MINERALS

Our bodies need seven major minerals, plus further 'trace' or minor minerals.

Major minerals include:

- Calcium – needed for muscle, heart and digestive system health. It builds bone, and supports synthesis and function of blood cells. It is found in dairy products, eggs, salmon, sardines (when canned with bones), green leafy vegetables, fromage frais and yoghurt, nuts and seeds. Ideally children should have three servings of calcium-rich food every day. This could include a glass of milk, a pot of yoghurt and a piece of cheese.

- **Phosphorus** is used in energy processing, and works to build bones and teeth, as well as cell membranes. It is provided by red meat, dairy, poultry, fish, bread and rice.
- **Potassium** – important for regulation of energy transfer. It is found in legumes, potato skin, tomatoes, bananas, papayas, lentils, dry beans, whole grains, yams, soybeans, spinach, chard, sweet potato and turmeric.
- **Sulphur** – used in the body's metabolic processes and a key part of keratin, found in our hair and skin. It comes from meat, eggs, poultry and fish: garlic, onions, wheat germ, kale and asparagus also contain sulphur.
- **Magnesium** – stored in bones and used for energy processing. It can be obtained from raw nuts and green vegetables.
- **Chlorine** – used to create stomach acid for digestion, found in salt.
- **Sodium** – important for regulation of energy transfer, found in salt, milk and spinach.

In a modern diet, salt is added to many processed foods, from crisps to ready meals and pre-cooked sauces. Too much salt isn't healthy. Don't add salt when cooking at home, and avoid processed foods with high levels of sodium. Watch out for bacon, ham, sausages and cheese as these are high in salt too. 1 g of salt is equivalent to 0.4 g of sodium. Babies should have no added salt in their diets. 1–3-year-olds should have less than 2 g, 4–6-year-olds less than 3 g, 7–10-year-olds less than 5 g and 11–18 year olds less than 6 g.

Trace minerals include:

- **Iron** – needed to make up many proteins and enzymes. It keeps red blood cells healthy and is found in red meat, liver, fortified cereal, grains, beans, pulses, eggs, spinach, chard, turmeric, cumin, parsley, lentils, tofu, asparagus, salad greens, soybeans, shrimp, beans, tomatoes and olives.
- **Cobalt** – a key part of vitamin B12.
- **Copper** – found in mushrooms, spinach, greens, seeds, raw cashews, raw walnuts, tempeh and barley.

- **Zinc** – which helps many body functions. It is found in eggs, dry beans, mushrooms, spinach, asparagus, scallops, red meat, peas, yoghurt, oats and seeds.
- **Molybdenum** – found in some vegetables, eggs, sunflower seeds, wheat flour, lentils and cereal grain.
- **Iodine** – used in thyroid hormones and as an antioxidant. It is found in sea vegetables, iodized salt and eggs.
- **Selenium** – which helps antioxidant enzymes function. It is found in Brazil nuts, cold-water wild fish (cod, halibut, salmon), tuna, lamb, turkey, calf liver, mustard, mushrooms, barley, cheese and garlic.
- **Manganese** – which is used in enzyme functions. It is found in spelt grain, brown rice, beans, spinach, pineapple, tempeh, rye, soybeans, thyme, raspberries, strawberries, garlic, squash, eggplant and cloves.

There are further minerals that we know have a role in human health, but it is currently unclear what they do; then there are others that probably have a role, but have yet to have this proven. Many vitamins and minerals need to be consumed as part of a healthy diet in order to be effective. For example, iron is absorbed more effectively when combined with vitamin C from citrus fruits or juice.

How we eat

Ingestion, digestion and egestion are the words that describe the way we take food and liquids in through our mouths, how we process them, how we absorb the nutrients and how waste products eventually leave the body. It is a complex system, but for most people this process takes place without issues. Read on to learn more about normal digestion.

Food and liquids enter into our bodies through the **mouth**. Babies use their tongues to move milk from the front to the back of their mouths. This is called **suckling**. Seemingly a natural instinct for survival, in fact suckling is a complex combination of extension and retraction of the tongue, and forward and backward jaw movements, co-ordinated with closure of the lips around the mother's nipple.

As the first months pass, the baby develops the strength to move from suckling to **sucking**. This rhythmic up and down movement includes firmer closure of the lips around the nipple, leading to negative pressure in the baby's mouth. At this stage (around four to six months) many parents start to introduce first foods. It takes time for the infant to learn how to move food through their mouth with their tongue, and to develop a rhythmic 'bite and release' pattern. As infants develop **teeth** they can learn to take in **solid food** which is chewed to a paste with **saliva** to form a **bolus**.

Saliva comes from **salivary glands.** Saliva is 99.5% water, combined with electrolytes, mucus, glycoproteins, enzymes and anti-bacterial compounds. Enzymes in saliva play a vital role in starting digestion of carbohydrates and fats. The same enzymes also protect the teeth by breaking down trapped food. The other role of saliva is to lubricate food to make it easy to **swallow** and to protect the mouth from drying out.

Controlling the movement of food with the tongue while moving the jaw up and down is known as **munching** and enables a child to deal with more solid food. The child also needs to be able to move food from side to side with the tongue to develop a **mature rotary chew** co-ordinating vertical, lateral and diagonal movement with closed lips.

Swallowing is the process of passing something from the **mouth** to the **pharynx** to the oesophagus. At the same time, the **epiglottis** folds down to prevent food getting into the trachea and lungs. Swallowing involves a complex set of movements. The first part, the oral phase, is voluntary: that is, the person initiates it at will. Movement of the bolus of food to touch receptors in the pharynx starts the pharyngeal phase. This and the oesophageal phase are reflexes, controlled automatically by the autonomic nervous system. The oesophagus has two main jobs. It is made of a tube of muscles that contract in sequence in a movement called **peristalsis** to push food and liquids from the mouth to the stomach. Alongside this downwards movement, the oesophagus also has three constrictions or **sphincters** which stop the stomach contents flowing back upwards, known as **reflux.**

From the oesophagus, foods and liquids move into the stomach.

The stomach contains space for food to be stored while it is combined with digestive enzymes, disintegrated and then released gradually. The stomach of a new baby can hold 60–90 ml, while an adult stomach can hold up to a litre. The stomach releases enzymes that digest protein, known as proteases, and acid to kill or inhibit bacteria and provide the right climate for the proteases to work. The muscles in the stomach wall contract in a movement called **peristalsis** to disintegrate the food bolus into **chyme** (partially digested food) which is then released into the **duodenum** by passing through the pyloric sphincter. The duodenum is the first part of the **small intestine**. At this stage, the body begins to extract nutrients from the chyme. It can take from forty minutes to a few hours for the food to be digested, depending on the type of food.

The **small intestine** is a long tube with strong muscle walls. The first part of it is called the duodenum, the second part the **jejunum**, and the third part the **ileum**. Within this area, partially digested food is mixed with secretions from the **pancreas**, the **liver**, and the **intestinal glands**. This allows the body to absorb nutrients such as vitamins, trace elements, fluids and electrolytes, as each component of food is turned into its smallest component parts. The inner surface of the small intestine is covered with tiny 'fingers' called **villi** and **micro villi**. These increase the surface area, maximizing food absorption.

The **large intestine**, or **colon**, is a continuation of the small intestine. Within the large intestine, any remaining water and electrolytes are absorbed into the body. Finally, any remaining waste from the digested food passes into the **rectum** which holds the waste until it can be **egested**.

Other parts of the body have important functions to aid digestion too. The **liver** aids the metabolism of protein and carbohydrate and stores glycogen and vitamins. It also aids in the formation, storage and elimination of bile and plays a role in fat metabolism. The **gallbladder** is a tiny sac that rests on the liver. It collects bile, which is essential for the digestion and absorption of fats, from the liver. The **pancreas** creates secretions which help balance the acidity of the partly digested food (chyme) from the stomach. These secretions are also important in the absorption of fats, proteins and carbohydrates.

Summary

This chapter has helped you understand more about healthy eating. You may want to pick one or more of the following actions to take, depending on which is suitable for your child:

- ✓ Try different foods. Pick one food to try and give every family member the chance to taste, lick or sniff the food. Present the food a number of times so people can get used to it.
- ✓ Eat together as much as possible. Your child will learn from seeing you eat a range of healthy food.
- ✓ Don't exclude foods unless necessary.
- ✓ Think about healthy alternatives you can offer to fatty or sugary treats.
- ✓ Offer water to drink as a first choice. Don't let children drink fizzy or sugary drinks.

Chapter 2
When Eating Goes Wrong

If your child has eating issues or you suspect issues are emerging it can be stressful. Eating issues are relatively common and are particularly common in children with special needs. This chapter will explore the implications of eating issues for a child and their family. Reasons for eating issues will begin to be explored and expert advice will be given to identify what you should do if you are worried about your child's eating.

Sometimes it is difficult to know when you need to seek advice. Dr Pippa Rundle specializes in child and baby development, and she offers the following advice:

" *Mealtimes should be welcome and harmonious events within a family. However, there are various issues that may cause parents to be anxious and concerned about their children's eating habits. These issues are most often related to: eating too little or too much, difficulty with chewing or swallowing, being very fussy or eating very slowly.*

If a child is eating a reasonably varied diet for his or her age and is maintaining weight and height there is seldom any need to worry. However, professional advice should generally be requested if weight gain is significantly above or below the norm. Parents should also be concerned if there is a reluctance to chew and swallow lumpy foods when these have been introduced. Children can gain attention at mealtimes by being unduly fussy, and by eating slowly. It is well worth seeking advice at an early stage, before these traits become more permanent. **"**

For more information about Dr Rundle's work visit www. drrundle.co.uk.

Issues for families

Eating difficulties can provide families with a range of problems and if you are feeling stressed about the problems that your child is having around food you are not alone. If your child isn't eating it can be extremely worrying and at times frustrating to deal with.

Sarah has a son with Asperger's syndrome who has recently developed issues with food:

" *I am so worried about Charlie; he eats so little that I'm concerned about his growth. I've also noticed that he is lacking in energy and I'm sure this is directly linked to his eating issues. I've got to the stage where I dread mealtimes now as I know that there will be an issue around food. He has become obsessed about reading food labels and is restricting his diet considerably. It's very frustrating at times as I just want him to eat yet I feel that if I mention food I'm making an issue out of the problem. I'm giving him vitamins to try to make up for his lack of nutrients. My husband is less patient than me and can get angry about his eating. I think we are going to seek medical advice as I can see his weight dropping day by day. I feel like such a failure for not being able to sort this out myself and I'm almost embarrassed to be going to the doctors with this issue; I mean, what can they do in all honesty if he refuses to eat?* "

Sarah's feelings are extremely common. You may experience a range of emotions about your child's feeding issues that can range from feeling empathic towards them to feeling frustrated that they won't eat. Couples can often disagree as well about how to handle the eating issue and this can be extremely difficult if the issue is behaviour-based. It is important that if you are parenting as a couple you take time out to discuss your thoughts and feelings when your child is not around. You may not always agree on the right way to deal with the problem but you should negotiate until you are able to reach a suitable compromise. If you are finding that the issues are beginning to impact on your relationship it is important that you acknowledge this and spend some time talking to each other openly and honestly. It is very easy to get so immersed in trying to manage your child's needs that you forget about your own. If you feel that you need somebody to talk to you could explore the option of couple's counselling. Your GP may be able to make a referral if necessary or alternatively you could contact a private counsellor, although a fee would be involved. You may also wish to explore Relate for Parents and Families, which is a website that offers support and access to online chat with a Relate counsellor. For more information about this service log on to www.relateforparents.org.uk.

Being a parent is very stressful; it becomes even more stressful when your child has special needs and an eating issue. It is important that you recognize that you are under a great deal of stress and that the feelings that you are having are justified. In Chapter 9 we will explore ways of dealing with stress.

Families are affected by feeding issues in many different ways, depending on the actual issue. It may be that you can't go out to restaurants any longer, or you have to plan meals with great precision to ensure that your child does not come into contact with food that they are allergic to, for example. Other families may have to tube-feed their child if medical issues play a role. However your family is affected it is important to acknowledge the issues and talk about them together.

If your child has siblings they too may be affected by the eating issue. You could find that you need to take your child with the eating issue to numerous appointments, you may need to research the condition more fully and you may find that you have more pressure on your time. Make sure that you set time aside for your other children too so that they don't feel excluded. Sibs is a UK charity that is set up to support the needs of those growing up with a brother or sister with additional needs. The Sibs website is packed full of useful information about how to support siblings through difficult times – log on to www.sibs.org.uk.

It is important that you do always answer siblings' questions about eating issues honestly. This will help them to understand more thoroughly what is going on. It will also help your other children to accept the difficulty in a more understanding manner.

The variety of appointments you may have to attend with your child with eating issues can bring you into contact with a wide range of professionals and specialists. Attending appointments can be an additional stress at a time when you are already feeling the pressure. Here are some tips to help you to manage appointments more easily:

✓ Make sure that you write down the date, time and venue of the appointment as soon as you receive the information. It is so easy to forget appointments, particularly when you are busy.

✓ Leave yourself plenty of time to get to appointments. Rushing to get there on time will mean that you arrive feeling stressed.

✓ Take somebody with you if at all possible. Sometimes you can find that there is too much information to take in or you may find it hard to concentrate on what is being said if you are also supervising your child. Taking a partner, family member or friend can be really helpful as it will free you up to listen to what is being said and they will also help you to recall information afterwards.

✓ Write a list of questions to take with you to the appointment. You may find that your mind goes blank once you enter the room.

✓ Write down the name of the person that you have seen and make sure that you get their contact details in case you need to get hold of them in the future. Also write down what their role is to remind you. Sometimes you may see a lot of different professionals and it can get very confusing.

✓ If you don't understand something then you should ask the professional to explain it again. Don't be worried about asking for clarification, not understanding doesn't mean that you are stupid: it may mean that they haven't explained it clearly!

Dr Rundle offers this advice:

❝ *When attending the initial meeting, it is useful if you can take details of the birth and medical history. Also remember to take the height and weight charts as given to you by your health visitor. A short food diary of exactly what your child has eaten and drunk over the last two or three days is helpful; this should be written at the time as snacks can get forgotten. It is also essential to know how and where meals are presented and by whom. Is the behaviour the same when staying with grandparents or out with friends? Is it different when parents are present?* ❞

While meetings with professionals can seem daunting you should always remember that you are the expert on your child. Try to remain positive about appointments and view them as a way of moving towards easing the problems that your child is experiencing at the moment.

Issues for your child

Your child will also have issues that need to be addressed if they are not able to eat appropriately. Some children may be very aware of their food issues and this can cause them to try to hide their problem or to be upset if it is broached. Your child's weight or growth may be affected and this may also cause them distress. If your child isn't eating enough they could be lethargic and their concentration may be impacted, which can lead to issues at school.

David is fifteen years old now and on the autism spectrum. He tells us:

" *I knew that I was getting fat, my tummy wobbled when I walked. We had a lesson at school about food and the teacher said that fat was bad for you. I then started to make sure that I didn't eat things with a lot of fat in them. I got very stressed at mealtimes and only wanted to eat fruit and vegetables. My parents didn't understand why but that was just the way it had to be. I've been to CAMHS (Child and Adolescent Mental Health Services) and I've done a lot of work about this and now realize that some fats are good for you too. I still restrict what I eat but not as much as I used to. I feel better now that I'm eating a healthy diet, I've got more energy to play football with my friends.* **"**

If your child can verbalize their feeding issues then it is important that they are given the time and space to do so. They need to feel that they are supported rather than judged. Some children may find it easier to speak to somebody outside of the family initially such as a teacher or health care professional, or there may be specialist coun-sellors in your area who can help. Ask your GP for details.

Feeding issues from birth

Feeding issues can occur throughout childhood but can be particularly worrying for new parents. There are a number of feeding issues that babies may suffer from including:

✓ Colic
✓ Constipation
✓ Vomiting or regurgitating
✓ Failure to thrive by poor weight gain
✓ Abdominal pain/wind
✓ Difficulties latching onto the breast

Penny Lazell runs www.healthvisitor4u.com, a private health visiting and children's sleep service. Penny is a registered general nurse and health visitor. She is also a qualified midwife and neonatal nurse. Penny shares her advice with us:

" *Department of Health guidelines state that babies should be exclusively breast- or bottle-fed until six months of age; however, in some situations you may be advised to start your baby on solid foods before this by a health professional, for instance, babies with gastro-oesophageal reflux or babies who are failing to thrive organically. Most babies over six months of age will be happy to take food off a spoon and also start to feed themselves. They are also able to cope with lumpier foods as their chewing skills should be well developed by this stage.*

Babies with additional needs may often have trouble moving on to lumpier foods for a number of reasons. If they have any sort of sensory issues the oral cavity is top of the list as this area is hypersensitive and babies and children have big issues with new tastes and textures and often become very fussy eaters. They tend to start refusing lumpier foods, preferring the smooth tastes and textures they have been used to. They will often start to gag on the lumpier foods; this can be quite frightening and parents will often revert back to purées again. This in turn delays the development of chewing skills. If your baby gets to eight to nine months of age and is reluctant to take lumpier foods or attempt to self-feed it would be a good idea to talk to your health visitor to assess whether it is a problem or not. "

If you are concerned about your baby's feeding it is important that you get medical advice. Many feeding issues in infancy are resolved quickly but you should always speak to your health visitor if you are concerned. A health visitor is a registered nurse or midwife who has undertaken further training – the role involves improving the health of children in the early years and supporting their families. Your health visitor will not only be able to offer advice and signpost you on to appropriate professionals if necessary, they will also be able to monitor your baby's weight and growth.

Penny offers the following advice:

" *You can encourage your baby or child to become happier and more familiar with foods by letting them play with food and self-feed as much as possible. Initially it may seem that nothing is going in but over time, once they become familiar with the texture and smell of the food, they will probably start putting it to their lips and then actually putting it in the mouth. Try to avoid putting food into the mouth yourselves. It is important that babies and children are allowed to use their senses of touch, smell and sight to become familiar with food. Try eating together so your child gets the idea that eating is fun rather than a lonely experience sitting in front of a TV. This also often slows down the eating process, allowing the child to be able to chew their food properly, which reduces gagging and aids digestion. Give babies and children very small portions; a big plate of food can often feel quite intimidating, and remember: the messier they get the more fun they are having!* "

Fussy eating

Melissa Hood is director of the Parent Practice. She tells us:

" *When parents of small children have concerns around their children's eating it tends to fall into the category of fussy eating, that is they're not eating enough, or they only like a narrow range of foods and these aren't the most healthy ones, or they develop an annoying insistence on eating only 'white foods' or 'square' foods or won't mix different foods on one plate, or will only eat off the Star Wars plate and so on. According to the Royal College of Psychiatrists a third of under-fives develop some sort of food fad, either food refusal or selective eating, which makes it a pretty normal part of development. There's even a name for this childhood development stage. It is called neophobia where children develop a fear of new things, in this case food.* "

Read more about neophobia in Chapter 4.

" *The peak period for fads is probably around two to three years old when children start wanting to exercise some control and exert some independence in their lives. This period often coincides with the arrival of new siblings, the start of nursery school, the move into a big bed, or out of a high-chair, and it is also the peak age for developing a fear of new things. Even children previously thought of as good eaters can start rejecting any new food and even refuse familiar foods they once enjoyed, which is really frustrating for parents.* "

Melissa goes on to explain:

" *Most recent research shows that even the fussiest of fussy eaters are highly likely to meet, perhaps even exceed, the recommended energy and dietary intake for their age group. Even when it seems to us they are eating totally random and strange things, and never sit still long enough to eat anything of note, they continue to grow and develop. If you are concerned about their vitamin intake give them a multivitamin to reduce your anxiety around food. This is important because parental anxiety is at the root of most mealtime battles.* "

Feeding issues and nursery or school

If your child is a little older and you are worried about their eating when they attend school or nursery it is important to share this with the educational setting. Schools are used to working with children who have a wide range of feeding issues and should work with you to ensure that the difficulty is dealt with in an appropriate manner.

Charlotte Stirling-Reed is a registered public health nutritionist and an expert in paediatric nutrition. Charlotte has worked with many schools, children centres and nurseries, helping them to improve the foods they offer to the children who attend. Charlotte also works privately with parents and runs training for health care professionals on topics such as weaning, general healthy eating and fussy eating. Charlotte believes that schools and child care facilities can and should do a huge amount to help improve the nutrition of young children as well as providing support for parents to enable them to feed their children appropriately.

Charlotte tells us:

" *When children spend a lot of their time in school during the day, it is hard to really know what is going on and how their eating is progressing. Make sure you keep up good communication with your child's teacher and head teacher and ask if they are happy to provide you with some feedback at the end of the school day. It is also important to explain your child's food likes and dislikes right from the word go, so that teachers and staff are aware of what to look out for and how to deal with issues such as food refusal.* **"**

You can visit Charlotte's website at www.srnutrition.co.uk.

Sophie is mum to Destiny who is three years old, has cerebral palsy and is tube fed. Sophie tells us:

" *I presumed that Destiny would have to go to a special school because of her feeding issues. I was surprised when the Portage [a home educational service for pre-school children with special educational needs] home visitor said that she could attend nursery alongside her friends in our neighbourhood. I was really worried about how they would cope with her being tube fed but it has been fine. I had a long chat with the*

SENCO (Special Educational Needs Co-ordinator) prior to her starting school and they had staff trained by the school nurse so that they knew how to administer feeds. A care plan was put in place which was signed and agreed by everyone involved. The staff have been fantastic and Destiny is fully included in all the activities within the nursery. My advice to other parents is to speak to the school about the issues and explore together how they can be overcome. **"**

It is important that you share any concerns or issues around feeding with your child's school as soon as possible. Schools work with a range of professionals who will be able to offer them advice and support. Ask to speak to the Special Educational Needs Co-ordinator. Explain to them exactly what the eating issues are and what your concerns are. Sometimes writing down what you are going to say before the meeting can be helpful to make sure that you don't forget to share any information. The outline below can help you to think about what kind of information you need to share:

✓ What exactly is the eating issue?
✓ How long has your child had the eating issue?
✓ What are your concerns about their eating when at school?
✓ Which professionals have been involved with your child to date?
✓ How can the school help to resolve your concerns?

If you have any medical reports regarding the eating issue it is also helpful to take copies of these to the meeting to share. The sooner you share this information with the school the better, as sometimes they need to arrange for experts such as speech and language therapists to offer feeding training to staff, which can take time and may delay your child's transition into the setting.

If your child is on a self-restricted diet or is simply eating very little, you may wish to consider whether it would be more appropriate to send a packed lunch for them, rather than arranging school dinners. Packed lunches can be helpful in that you can guarantee that your child will be provided with something that they may eat during the school day. They can also be useful in terms of checking on how much your child has eaten as the remnants will be in the box.

Teresa Bliss is an educational psychologist and recognizes how stressful it can be for parents if their child has an eating issue. Here she offers her expert advice on how to deal with schools.

" *If your child is a fussy eater then you should arrange for your child to take a packed lunch with food that they will actually eat. In the case of younger children ensure that they can manage the packaging, for example, opening yoghurt pot tops. Tell the class teacher about your child's difficulties with food. Explain that you are ensuring a balanced diet, and supplement with vitamins if necessary. Be clear with the school about how you want your child's eating managed, particularly by lunchtime staff. Forcing the child to eat is never a good idea. Encouragement and patience are far more effective. Initially you will need to speak to the class teacher; ask the class teacher if they would like you to talk to the head teacher who is the person most likely to supervise lunchtime staff.*

Many schools follow the government 'healthy schools' strategy. This involves learning about food and how necessary a range of foods are to our health and well-being. It may be that this will help to change your child's attitude to food. Most state schools offer fruit at break time, teachers encourage children to try a variety of fruits, also the influence of peers eating a range of foods can have a positive impact on some children. Many parents report that their children's friends have had an influence, for better or worse, on their child's eating habits. **"**

Teresa also points out how important it is to take time to listen to children:

" *Listen to your child, be sure you understand what it is they dislike about certain foods. For example, some children are affected not only by a taste but also by texture and smell. Some children will only eat dry food such as cereal without milk; this is because they dislike the texture of cereal when it has become soggy. Some children enjoy school meals and feeding difficulties are resolved when they are allowed to have school lunches.*

What works at school is best approached as a trial and error process. Try to remain calm: higher emotional states are going to be less effective in terms of encouraging a child to eat than a calmer approach. I have known children survive on what appears to be amazingly small amounts of food, and following self-imposed restricted diets. When parents become distressed it only makes matters worse, and it is the same at school. The adults need to remain calm. "

If you are not happy with the school's suggestions around your child's eating issues you should speak to the head teacher in the first instance. You may wish to contact your local Parent Partnership service; this is an organization that offers information, advice and support to parents and carers of children with special educational needs. Their role is to support parents in having their views understood and you may be offered support when attending meetings. The Parent Partnership service is a voluntary organization that provides confidential and impartial advice. To find out more about their role and to locate your nearest service log on to www.parentpartnership.org.uk.

Social issues and eating

Eating tends to be a social occasion. Generally speaking, people enjoy eating together and food is something that is to be shared. Mealtimes have always been events that have drawn people together right through the ages. We celebrate many occasions through food such as birthday parties, wedding breakfasts and Christmas dinner.

Some children find the social side of eating extremely distressing. Children who, for example, have sensory issues can find dining with others far too challenging; the noise levels may be distressing, particularly in a large restaurant or even a school dining hall. The smells may be overpowering and the general busyness of the environment can be upsetting. Some children benefit from wearing ear defenders to help with the noise issue and find that they can then tolerate social dining.

Jessica is six years old and has sensory issues. Her mum tells us:

❝ *Jessica has a complex sensory profile and can find busy situations over-stimulating. I never thought that she would be able to tolerate eating in a busy social environment because of this. She is particularly sensitive to noise and after researching about sensory issues I decided to buy a pair of ear defenders to try out. They made an immediate difference to her ability to function. She uses them in the dining hall at school now and she can sit alongside her friends and eat her meal; before, she would become very upset. Her friends just accept that she wears them as she needs them. Since we introduced these she has started to access more social eating situations and I can, for example, now take her into a café, a scenario I would have previously avoided at all cost.* **❞**

Others may have issues that mean they genuinely fear being watched whilst eating. Social Anxiety Disorder, for example, can begin in childhood and is a disorder which leads sufferers to have an irrational fear of being watched. This can be particularly difficult for sufferers around mealtimes and they may prefer to dine alone. Children on the autism spectrum may also have social issues around food. These will be explored more fully in Chapter 6.

If your child finds eating in social situations challenging it is important that you acknowledge this and try to ascertain what it is about the social situation that is causing them distress. Sometimes it is impossible to work this out but you may notice that they can cope in certain situations yet not others. If this is the case, see if you can ascertain whether, for example, one situation is not as noisy or perhaps as busy as the other. If you can work out what the trigger is then you can look at strategies to alleviate the problem. You cannot force a child to eat and trying to do so will only result in exacerbating the problem. Children like to feel that they are in control so it can be helpful to offer them a choice of two scenarios: you either eat in the dining room or at the kitchen table, for example.

Social Stories were developed by Carol Gray and are useful in describing a concept to children with additional needs. Many special schools use the idea of Social Stories to teach children information in a simple to understand yet reassuring manner. The goal of Social

Stories is not to change the behaviour but to improve understanding around the events that are causing issues that then will hopefully lead the child to demonstrate a more appropriate response.

Social Stories can be written around a host of subjects but lend themselves well to being used when a child has issues around eating socially. You could write a story for your child around situations that currently cause them distress to help them to develop their understanding of the situation further. For example, you could write about a meal in a restaurant, a birthday party or eating in school. For more information about Social Stories and how to write them visit www.thegraycenter.org.

Behaviour and eating issues

Many eating issues are behavioural, although it is important that you do rule out medical reasons for your child's feeding issues first.

Behavioural issues around food can manifest themselves in many different ways including:

✓ Gagging and vomiting
✓ Refusal to eat certain foods
✓ Spitting out food or milk
✓ Refusal to chew or swallow food
✓ Reluctance to try new food
✓ Refusal to sit at a dining table
✓ Tantrums, screaming and crying at mealtimes
✓ Throwing food

There can be many reasons why behavioural issues around food begin and these can include children having had an aversive feeding issue that has left them with a negative association around food, such as an episode of choking or vomiting. Developmental delay can be another reason for behavioural issues. Typically, children aged twelve to fourteen months may display behavioural issues around food and mealtimes, whereas children with additional needs may display these behaviours at a later stage.

Food intake is one area of a child's life where they can take control.

It is therefore a common one for children to develop behavioural issues around. If it is suspected that your child's issue around food is a behavioural one it is important to stay calm; getting angry can escalate the issue. Seeking advice can be important and also developing a support network for yourself: it can be very stressful dealing with these kinds of issues on a daily basis.

Your role as a parent is key in working through behavioural issues with food. Try to present your child with appropriate foods in a non-threatening way: you are not forcing them to eat the food. Remember that bribery too is counterproductive; it is good to reward your child but don't ever attempt to bribe them. We will discuss appropriate rewards and incentive strategies in Chapter 8. You should aim to offer your child a relaxed, calm environment in which to eat their meals. Children with special needs are very tuned in to the stress of their parents. Even if you feel stressed at mealtimes try to take some deep breaths and smile. Praise their efforts when they do eat something and ignore the food that they have left. Mealtimes need to be made a positive experience for the whole family.

If you feel angry and frustrated around mealtimes, you are not alone. Many parents that we have spoken to said that they found their feelings spiralling out of control at times or that they dreaded mealtimes approaching. It is extremely important that you keep calm as you are aiming to provide a relaxed environment for eating. Your child will pick up on your stress and this can make their behaviour escalate. If you feel yourself losing control you should try to take some deep breaths until you feel in control once more. If it is safe to do so you may need to walk away from the situation for a few minutes until you regain your composure. It can also help to use self-talk to keep yourself calm when under pressure; Jane shares her tips with us here:

" *I get so wound up at times with Ruby, her eating drives me to distraction. I just want to yell at her which I know is the wrong thing to do. I find that I almost have to distract myself away from her behaviour by counting backwards in my head in threes from a hundred, or at other times I use a little chant that goes 'when life's getting you down a bit, rest for a while but don't you quit'. It sounds ridiculous but it is these strategies that have really helped me get by and stopped me losing it with her when the going gets tough!* "

It is also important to provide children who have behavioural issues around food with good role models. You could ask at school to see if your child can be seated at lunchtime with children who enjoy eating their meals. When at home it is important that they see you eating appropriately too as they learn directly from your behaviour what is and isn't appropriate. You should eat the same food as your child as this will encourage them to try different things. Sitting at a table with them also shows them how to behave at mealtimes and they will hopefully follow your lead. Children love attention and need to learn that they can get attention in ways other than around food. When you chat to your child while they are eating make sure that the conversation is steered away from food and talk about things that motivate them. Read Chapter 4 for more advice on selective eating.

Children thrive when they are treated with a consistent approach. It is important that you get into a routine around mealtimes so that they know what to expect and what is expected of them. Having a set routine can help children with special needs feel more secure and predict what is going to happen next. In Chapter 9 we will discuss visual timetables in detail; these can be helpful in developing a good mealtime routine. Try to stick to doing things in the same order and giving them some warning that mealtimes are going to begin. Decide as a family what is and is not reasonably acceptable at mealtimes and make sure that your child is aware of these limits.

In summary

There are a huge range of different eating issues and in this chapter we have focused more on the behavioural and social aspects associated with eating. You have read about other parents' stories and heard advice from professionals about how to proceed. In the next chapter we will be looking at the physical issues around eating problems.

Chapter 3
Physical and Physiological Problems with Normal Digestion

There are many issues that can cause children to have problems with digestion. Some are immediately obvious from birth while others take time to diagnose. As a parent it can help to understand more about what is behind each condition, so you understand why problems occur and what might help your child. Always talk to a medical practitioner about your child's individual issues before starting any treatment or change in diet.

Three of the most common issues for any parent are vomiting, diarrhoea and constipation, so this chapter starts with these conditions. Learn about what most children experience at some point in childhood, and when these may be a symptom of something more serious.

This chapter then looks at some medical conditions that can cause short- or long-term issues with digestion, including gastro-oesophageal reflux disorder, irritable bowel syndrome, Hirschsprung's disease, cleft lip and palate, dysphagia and intussusception.

Vomiting

Most children vomit at some point in childhood; some seem more prone to vomiting than others. Vomiting can be a normal response to a number of triggers, but it can also be the sign of more serious problems.

Complex messages to the brain tell our bodies to vomit for reasons ranging from motion sickness, the gag reflex (which protects us from swallowing things that are too large), irritation of the inner lining of the intestines, through to stress.

Before vomiting, retching takes place when the abdominal muscles contract together with the diaphragm and muscles used in inspiration (inhalation). Vomiting takes place alongside increased production of saliva to protect the teeth from stomach acid. At the same time, the body breathes in to avoid breathing at the same time as vomiting. Then the food is moved up from the middle of the small intestine into the stomach, increasing pressure, which then drives it into the oesophagus and out of the mouth. After vomiting the body releases endorphins which can make the person feel better.

Vomiting is often caused by illness – 'stomach flu' covers a wide range of bacteria and viruses that cause gastric inflammation. Vomiting is a way for the body to get rid of what it sees as potentially harmful substances.

Vomiting can also be caused by many different issues such as:

✓ Food allergies
✓ Lactose intolerance
✓ Food poisoning
✓ Motion sickness
✓ Migraine
✓ Infections such as ear or urinary tract
✓ Concussion
✓ Benign intracranial hypertension and hydrocephalus
✓ Chemotherapy

If your child is sick, offer water or an oral rehydration drink once they have finished vomiting. Small sips or spoonfuls of drink are better: a large drink may simply come back up. You may offer plain foods, but many children don't feel like eating at this stage.

Talk to NHS Direct or your GP if you are concerned about your child vomiting, especially if they are floppy, irritable and less responsive, if they have a headache or a stiff neck, or if vomiting lasts more than a couple of days. Occasionally vomiting can lead to dehydration. According to NHS Direct, symptoms of dehydration in children include:

✓ Appearing to get more unwell
✓ Being irritable or drowsy
✓ Passing urine infrequently

✓ Pale or mottled skin
✓ Cold hands and feet

Consult a medical practitioner if your child shows these symptoms. If your child vomits regularly, this can lead to long-term malnutrition and can affect their growth and development. Some children with additional needs also have problems with digestion that can make them more prone to vomiting. Read on for more information about specific conditions, and always consult your doctor if you feel that your child's vomiting might be related to something more serious.

Diarrhoea

Many children experience short bouts of diarrhoea. Diarrhoea can vary from slightly runny stools to extremely liquid bowel movements accompanied by stomach pain. Sometimes this can be accompanied by vomiting, a raised temperature and headaches. Children with diarrhoea will often need to get to the toilet urgently.

Most commonly, diarrhoea is caused by a virus, such as a norovirus or rotavirus, bacteria, or parasites infecting the intestines. Children may be more prone to diarrhoea if they put their hands in their mouth regularly.

Some children may produce diarrhoea if they are under stress. It can also be a side effect of some medications including antibiotics.

While most cases of diarrhoea resolve themselves, talk to your GP urgently if you have a child who has had six or more episodes of diarrhoea in a twenty-four-hour period. According to NHS Direct, you should also contact your GP if your child has:

✓ Diarrhoea and is vomiting at the same time
✓ Diarrhoea that is particularly watery
✓ Diarrhoea that has blood in it
✓ Diarrhoea that lasts for longer than two weeks

If your child has diarrhoea, you can help them by offering small regular drinks of water to avoid dehydration.

Your GP or pharmacist may recommend oral rehydration drinks if your child appears at risk of dehydration. According to NHS Direct, dehydration is an issue for children who:

✓ Are less than two years old and were born with a low birth weight
✓ Have had more than five episodes of diarrhoea in the last twenty-four hours
✓ Have vomited more than twice in the last twenty-four hours
✓ Have not been able to hold down fluids
✓ Have suddenly stopped breastfeeding

If your child is not dehydrated you can offer them small regular meals.

If they do not want to eat, keep offering water. If your child is dehydrated concentrate on offering drinks rather than food.

Most children will have diarrhoea for less than five to seven days. If your child still has diarrhoea after two weeks seek medical advice: consult a doctor sooner if they appear to be becoming dehydrated (see above).

Do not give your child over the counter anti-diarrhoea medications as these disguise problems rather than solve them.

Some toddlers are particularly prone to chronic diarrhoea. This can also relate to too many sugary drinks and too much fruit juice, especially between meals. If your toddler has a diet that is high in fibre, and has diarrhoea, you may want to reduce the amount of fibre in the diet.

There are other causes of diarrhoea including:

✓ Irritable bowel syndrome – see page 54
✓ Coeliac disease (intolerance to gluten)
✓ Crohn's disease (inflammation of the lining of the digestive system)
✓ Cystic fibrosis
✓ Lactose intolerance

Talk to your child's GP or specialist if you are concerned about these conditions.

Constipation

Although constipation can be an issue for any child, many children with special needs are more prone to constipation. It can be an issue in children with conditions from spina bifida to cerebral palsy to Down's syndrome.

Some doctors may define constipation as occurring simply when your child has fewer stools than they usually do. Others define it as less than three bowel movements a week. Stools tend to be hard and dry, with pain and straining.

Constipation can be caused by:

✓ Eating too many processed foods that are low in fibre
✓ Not drinking enough
✓ Lack of exercise, which may be difficult for some children with special needs
✓ A child ignoring their body's signals to go to the toilet owing to absorption with other tasks
✓ Emotional issues such as:
  • Change in routine, such as not knowing where toilets are in a new school
  • Embarrassment at having a bowel movement in public, such as using school toilets
  • Pressure to toilet train
  • Stress at school or home
✓ Repeated constipation, which can cause the child to avoid defecating because of discomfort. This desensitizes the bowel so the child is less likely to be aware they need to go in future
✓ Abnormal development of the intestines, rectum or anus
✓ Inadequate communication of the brain to the bowel in conditions where the nervous system is poorly developed or damaged
✓ Endocrine problems, such as hypothyroidism
✓ Some medications, including painkillers and iron supplements

You can tell your child is constipated if:

✓ Their stools are hard and dry
✓ They don't have a bowel movement for several days
✓ They are distressed in the bathroom or try to avoid bowel movements
✓ They have a painful bloated abdomen
✓ They lack interest in food in a way that is unusual for them
✓ They have dribbles of faecal matter in their underwear

There are some self-help methods that may assist children with constipation. Gradually add in foods that are high in fibre to your child's diet. Make sure that they drink plenty of water alongside high-fibre foods as this helps soften stools.

Healthy foods rich in fibre include:

✓ Wholemeal bread
✓ Vegetables
✓ Fruit
✓ Baked beans
✓ High-fibre cereal
✓ Nuts and beans

Adding an extra glass of fruit juice to your child's diet can help. Avoid caffeinated drinks such as cola, tea or coffee. Regular meals will help your child develop healthy bowel habits. Allow time after the meal for a bowel movement.

Gently increase the amount of exercise your child takes if you can. Exercise helps the intestines push food through.

Give your child the chance to sit on the toilet at least twice daily to encourage them to have a bowel movement. Make sure that they sit for up to ten minutes. After a meal is the ideal time. Give them a tick or star on a reward chart for each time they sit on the toilet if they are reluctant to comply.

Long-term constipation can cause serious problems for a child. Hard stools can irritate or tear the lining of the anus. If constipation is not resolved with a healthy diet, talk to your GP or paediatrician.

The doctor will ask about your child's medial history and diet. In a small number of children, further tests may be recommended to check whether there are problems with the bowel.

The doctor may recommend laxatives or stool softeners if the methods above do not help. Do not buy these drugs over the counter without medical advice: only use them if your child's doctor recommends them. Some children who have special needs that make them prone to constipation may find it better to use stool softeners or laxatives on a regular basis to avoid developing a fear of pain associated with bowel movements. For most children, however, constipation is only temporary.

David has been constipated since around nine months old. Recently he went fourteen days without a movement. Sheila says:

" *He had been on lactulose, but it had stopped helping. The paediatrician suggested phosphate enemas to remove the blockage. This was tried four times in the hospital but without solving the issue so David was sent to a bigger local hospital where they performed a manual evacuation under general anaesthetic. The consultant tested for Hirschprung's disease while he was in there. But this came back negative. Since then we have been prescribed Movicol and sodium picosulphate and have been put under the care of a constipation nurse specialist. She's marvellous! She has increased the strength of the Movicol and comes in to see us every week or fortnight, depending on how well his condition is managed at the time. At the moment we've been using a half-dose of sodium picosulphate and he has had explosive bowel movements every morning, so we may reduce this slightly so he only goes every other day, as the drug gives him stomach cramps. We give it before bed, so he can sometimes wake in the middle of the night with pain.* "

David's constipation and autism are linked. Sheila says:

" *Both his brain and his gut seem to be delayed in developing. We've been told that it will take a year or more to get his gut back to normal once the constipation is resolved – at the moment it will be stretched and less sensitive to build-up as that is what he is used to, which means that his brain doesn't get the messages it needs.* 〝

Cleft lip and palate

Cleft palate is a congenital deformity – something a child is born with when the face doesn't develop properly before birth. It is associated with a number of syndromes including Fragile X, Stickler syndrome, Van Der Woude syndrome and Loeys Dietz syndrome. It can be treated successfully with surgery soon after birth, and recent advances have allowed it to be detected before birth in some cases. The cleft can simply be in the upper lip, or occur in the roof of the mouth, or both. Cleft can cause problems with feeding and speech. When feeding an infant prior to treatment, use an upright position to allow gravity to assist the flow of milk. There is also specialist feeding equipment available, but parents may prefer to simply select the most suitably shaped bottle insert, combined with a larger hole for easier delivery of milk and squeeze the bottle to increase the flow of milk.

Surgery usually takes place to repair a cleft lip at around ten weeks. The child will continue to be monitored by the craniofacial team as they grow to adulthood. Surgery for cleft palate will take place at around six to twelve months. The child may need bone grafting or orthodontic work from age nine into their teens.

Diabetes

Diabetes is a condition where the body is unable to metabolize glucose. In England and Wales 17 children per 100,000 develop diabetes each year. In Scotland the figure is 25 per 100,000.

In type 1 diabetes, the more common type in children, the body's immune system attacks insulin-producing cells. Without sufficient insulin, the level of glucose in the blood rises, and can damage all the organ systems in the body. If glucose is not processed your child will lack energy, and feel tired and unwell. The body will try to pass out excess glucose in the urine, and will use fat stores for energy, so key signs of diabetes are weight loss, thirst, extra urination and tiredness. Children can also complain of tummy pains and headaches, or have behavioural problems.

Diabetes can't be cured, but is treated by giving the body the insulin it needs, either by injection or pump. There are different types of insulin. Some act more quickly, and others have a longer action. Your consultant will work out what suits your child best. This can change as they grow up. In combination with a healthy diet and exercise, this can give your child a healthy life. Ask to speak to a dietitian about a good diet for your child.

Type 2 diabetes occurs when not enough insulin is produced, even though there are still some insulin-producing cells present. It is treated by changing to a healthier lifestyle, losing weight and increasing physical activity. Medication may be needed if these measures don't have enough effect.

There is a lot of information to take on board when your child is first diagnosed with diabetes, but organizations like Diabetes UK can help. Visit www.diabetes.org.uk.

Naomi's daughter was diagnosed with diabetes at the age of ten. She says:

What got us through the first few months was numbing the injection site first with ice before giving the injection. All the professionals were against this as it was supposed to make it a bit more difficult to get the needle in but we weighed this against being able to do the injection without tears. Once she was used to doing them herself she quite happily switched to not needing ice. The injections were almost the easiest part, only twice a day to start with. What was most traumatic was the finger pricking, which is painful, and needed doing several times a day. That would take up to an hour each time. What we found, and I'm not sure how, or who told us, was using the earlobe, the very bottom, for the blood testing. It's not only relatively painless (you pinch your ear now, you can barely feel it) but it's also conveniently located so the blood drops easily and nicely on to the blood testing strip. Yes you do end up with slightly bruised looking

*ears, though you do alternate them, and it is a small incon-
venience rather than having painful fingertips you can't use.
It does take some getting used to doing them yourself using
a mirror though she adapted to that quite quickly and deftly.
Again, the professionals frowned on it, saying it isn't that
accurate. I'm not sure how they reach that considering the
fingers are further away from the main circulatory system. In
any case, if a reading seems 'out' from how one is feeling it's
always best to do one again to double check which is a lot
easier to convince a little one to do on the earlobes as it's so
painless.* 〞

Dysphagia

Dysphagia is a condition that is defined as difficulty with swallowing
foods, where swallowing is often painful. A child with dysphagia will
struggle to pass food or liquid from the mouth by swallowing. The
problem takes place when one of the three phases of swallowing fails
to occur correctly – either when the tongue pushes food to the throat
after it has been chewed, or when the muscles in the throat (where the
epiglottis should close off the airways) relax and let food pass into
the oesophagus, or in the oesophageal phase where gravity helps
liquids fall into the stomach, and muscles push food towards the
stomach in waves known as peristalsis.

A number of health problems in children are associated with
dysphagia:

✓ Cleft lip or palate
✓ Conditions associated with a large tongue such as Down's
  syndrome and other chromosomal disorders
✓ Dental problems, such as when teeth do not meet properly
✓ Developmental delay
✓ Developmental problems with the bones and structures in the
  mouth
✓ Enlarged tonsils
✓ Gastro-oesophageal reflux disease leading to irritation or scarring
  of the oesophagus or vocal cords by acid

✓ Nerve and muscle diseases such as brain injury or muscular dystrophy

✓ Oesophageal compression by enlargement of other body parts, such as the heart, thyroid gland, blood vessels or lymph nodes

✓ Oral sensitivity in children who have been on a ventilator for a prolonged period of time

✓ Paralysis of the vocal cords

✓ Prenatal digestive tract malformations, such as oesophageal atresia

✓ Tracheostomy

✓ Tumours or masses in the face or throat such as in neuro-fibromatosis

Children with dysphagia may have problems with growth as they cannot take in enough food. Watch out for signs including:

✓ Complaints of a lump in the throat

✓ Coughing, choking or congestion after eating or drinking

✓ Difficulty sucking

✓ Dribbling

✓ Gagging

✓ One mouthful needing several attempts to swallow

✓ Pain in the throat or chest

✓ Regular chest infections

✓ Slow eating

✓ Tiredness or shortness of breath after eating or drinking

✓ Vomiting or sneezing regularly after eating

✓ Weight loss

Dysphagia can cause further problems if food is taken into the airways, leading to pneumonia. Talk to your paediatrician if you are concerned that your child has these symptoms. Your child may be referred for tests, which involve getting images of their throat and oesophagus taken using a liquid containing barium which shows up well on X-rays. Alternatively, they may need an endoscopy, where a small tube with a camera is passed into your child's throat and oesophagus under general anaesthetic. This tube may also be used to take samples.

Treatment for dysphagia will depend on the cause as well as your child's age, general health, other medical conditions and needs. You may be referred so that your child can work with a speech and language therapist. You may be advised about the best texture of food to offer your child: some children may find thickened fluids easier to swallow than runnier liquids. See Chapter 4 for advice for children who have oral hypersensitivity. Treating associated conditions, such as GORD (gastro-oesophageal reflux disease), will help with dysphagia. Some children with dysphagia will have long-term problems, particularly if the dysphagia is associated with other health problems, such as those that affect the nerves and muscles.

Gastro-oesophageal reflux disease (GORD)

Gastro-oesophageal reflux disease occurs when the muscle (the lower oesophageal sphincter) that should keep the stomach contents within the stomach is weak. Acid stomach contents can then drift back up into the oesophagus, causing heartburn and/or vomiting and breathing problems in some children.

Signs of GORD include:

- ✓ Burning chest pain, known as heartburn
- ✓ Burping
- ✓ Hiccups
- ✓ Stomach ache
- ✓ Vomiting regularly
- ✓ Fussiness or refusal to eat
- ✓ Gagging
- ✓ Choking
- ✓ Coughing
- ✓ Wheezing
- ✓ Sore throat

GORD symptoms are worse after eating, and can increase on lying down or bending over.

GORD is common in infants, but can occur at any age. It is more common in children with low muscle tone, both because this can cause the sphincter muscle to be weak and because the child may be less inclined to stay upright. It may be more likely to occur in children with Down's syndrome, cerebral palsy, autism, Fragile X and those who are born prematurely.

It causes a number of issues for children, including the following:

✓ Regular vomiting can mean that the child doesn't get as many calories as they need, which can impair growth
✓ Regular vomiting can damage teeth
✓ Acid can cause inflammation and ulcers in the oesophagus, which can bleed, leading to anaemia. Long-term inflammation can lead to a narrowed oesophagus
✓ Even if the child does not vomit, the risk is that acid can reach the windpipe, causing difficulties such as asthma, pneumonia and possibly sudden infant death syndrome

GORD can be worsened by certain foods: some people find high-fat foods increase the problem, while others are affected by peppermint or chocolate as these can relax the sphincter. Foods that increase stomach acid – citrus juices, fizzy drinks, spicy foods – can also increase the problem.

GORD can be diagnosed by a doctor who may carry out a chest X-ray. Your child may need to swallow a drink that includes barium, which shows up on an X-ray. An endoscope, a small flexible tube with a camera at the end, can be used to look inside the oesophagus. This may be done under general anaesthetic.

Some medications may worsen GORD – ask your doctor to review what your child is taking. Do not stop medications without medical advice.

For some children GORD can be managed with diet and lifestyle changes, such as:

✓ Cutting out fizzy drinks, peppermint, chocolate, fatty and spicy foods, acid foods and juices (citrus and tomatoes are particular offenders)
✓ Allowing children to eat small portions: physically this can lessen the chance of reflux. Compensate with regular small healthy snacks

✓ Timing meals so that your child doesn't lie down to sleep or nap right afterwards. A gap of two hours between the evening meal and bedtime can help

Beyond these changes, medication can help to cut down the amount of stomach acid produced, or help the stomach empty faster.

Your doctor may prescribe food supplements to help your child take on enough calories for healthy growth.

In infants where reflux is causing the baby to become tired before consuming enough, tube feeding may be recommended. See Chapter 6 for more about tube feeding.

In severe cases, the consultant may recommend an operation called fundoplication. This may be recommended if there is severe irritation in the oesophagus, frequent breathing problems, vomiting and lack of weight gain. The top part of the stomach is used to create a tight band to decrease reflux.

In the long term, many children outgrow GORD.

Hirschsprung's disease

Children with Hirschsprung's disease lack some of the nerve cells that should be in the intestinal wall. These do not form properly in utero, meaning that the intestines do not get the right messages from the brain to move food in a movement called peristalsis. Stools do not move as they should, causing dangerous blockages in the bowel. Most babies with Hirschsprung's disease only miss nerve cells in the last couple of feet of the bowel. The pressure from stools builds up, causing intestinal walls to thin. Bacterial infections can develop causing serious problems.

It's not known what causes the condition, but it happens in some-where between 1 in 4,000 and 1 in 7,000 births. Boys are more likely to have the condition than girls, and it is fifty times more likely to occur in a child with Down's syndrome. There is a familial link: if you have one baby with Hirschsprung's disease, there is a three to twelve per cent chance that a sibling will have the disease. If you have Hirschsprung's disease, there is an increased chance that your children will also have it.

The symptoms of Hirschsprung's disease show up within the first few weeks of life for most babies: less serious cases with fewer nerve cells missing may take longer to be diagnosed. Symptoms can vary from child to child but will include:

✓ No bowel movements within forty-eight hours of birth
✓ Increasingly bloated abdomen
✓ Vomiting
✓ Fever

If the condition does not become evident in early infanthood, children may also show:

✓ Worsening constipation/small watery stools
✓ Diminishing appetite
✓ Slow growth

If you are concerned about your child, talk to their medical practitioner as these symptoms can relate to a number of conditions.

If the doctor suspects Hirschsprung's disease, they may recommend that your child has an X-ray. Your child may need an enema that contains barium, which highlights the intestines on X-ray, showing up blockages, and narrowing or widened areas of the intestine. There are specific tests to measure nerve reflexes and/or the doctor may take a sample of cells.

Your child may need an operation to remove any bowel obstruction. At the same time the consultant is likely to remove the section of intestine that lacks nerve cells. Your child may be left with a colostomy, an opening in the abdomen attached to the intestines. Bowel movements pass through the opening into a collection bag which needs changing regularly. Some children only need a temporary colostomy, while for others it will be permanent depending on the location and amount of intestine removed.

In the long term, children who only have a temporary colostomy can experience frequent loose stools after the intestines are reconnected to the anus. This can lead to skin irritation, so clean carefully after bowel movement and consider using nappy cream if your child appears to be sore. Children may not know when they need to defecate, so make sure that they get the chance to sit on the toilet for around ten minutes after meals. Your child may need further help to have bowel movements. Your consultant can advise.

If a large part of the intestine has been removed because of lack of nerve cells, this reduces the area available for absorbing nutrients and liquid (See Chapter 1). Your consultant will advise on the best diet or necessary supplements for healthy growth. Your child will be advised to drink plenty of water.

Irritable bowel syndrome

Irritable bowel syndrome (IBS) is a condition which has a range of symptoms:

✓ Abdominal pain/discomfort
✓ Bloating
✓ Constipation
✓ Diarrhoea
✓ Flatulence
✓ Mucus in the stool
✓ Urgent need to pass a stool

Irritable bowel syndrome takes place when food doesn't pass properly through the intestines, causing pain, bloating, constipation or diarrhoea. Some children are more sensitive to changes in the intestine than others, and stress can also worsen symptoms. Around ten to fifteen per cent of children can have IBS. It occurs more often in children who have a parent with the condition, but there is no known genetic link.

The condition can be embarrassing for children, particularly if they need to use the toilet urgently. IBS itself can cause anxiety, which can in turn worsen the symptoms. The abdominal symptoms can be accompanied by headaches, nausea, dizziness and loss of appetite. IBS symptoms can be similar to other conditions such as GORD, diarrhoea and constipation, so take your child to the doctor to explore their particular symptoms. The doctor may carry out a range of tests to eliminate other causes of intestinal symptoms such as inflammation, infection or food allergies.

There are different options to treat IBS. If your child has lactose intolerance, restriction of lactose or enzyme supplements can reduce symptoms. Some children may find a high-fibre diet helps (see Chapter 1 for sources of dietary fibre), particularly if they are prone to constipation, but others will find this increases gas. Your doctor may be able to prescribe medication to help with IBS.

Intussusception

Intussusception is a condition that occurs when part of the intestines slips inside itself, like a folding telescope. This causes a blockage, and is the most common cause of intestinal obstruction in children between three months and six years old. Food can't pass through this section of bowel, causing the child to complain of pain followed by vomiting. Blood can't flow through the area either, which can damage the intestine, leading to infection or tissue death. Stools may appear normal initially, but then bloody stools may be accompanied by red mucus.

Intussusception occurs more often in children with cystic fibrosis (who are dehydrated), or after chemotherapy. It is also more likely to develop in children who already have intestinal or abdominal tumours, or who have gastroenteritis, or upper respiratory tract infections. It occurs more frequently in boys than girls.

It's not easy to detect whether your child's problems are caused by this condition, so consult your doctor. If your GP suspects intussusception they will refer your child to hospital where they will use X-rays to detect the abdominal obstruction. Your child may be given a barium enema, which will help show up the intestines on X-ray: the pressure from the barium liquid can also sometimes help resolve the intussusception. If your child is already seriously ill owing to abdominal infection, or has other complications, they may need surgery to unfold the intestines. Damaged sections of the intestine will be removed: if this is just a small section the ends will simply be sewn back together. If a large part of the intestine has been damaged your child may need a colostomy, where the end of the intestine is brought up to an opening in the wall of the abdomen and faecal matter passes into a bag. This may be temporary or permanent. If a large part of the intestine has been removed, your child may struggle to absorb enough nutrients from their food and may need supplements on a long-term basis to boost their calorie intake.

In summary

There are many different causes of digestive problems in children. Children with certain conditions, disabilities and additional needs may be more prone to digestive problems. Learn about your child's particular needs to help you manage their condition, and always talk to your medical practitioner to get advice relevant to your particular child.

Chapter 4
Selective Eating

Selective eating, fussy eating, picky eating … most parents meet this at some point in their child's life, but for some children this is more than just a stage that they will move through in a couple of years. In this chapter you can read about the different conditions that cause children to limit the food they eat, and what to do to help them. We will use the phrase selective eating to avoid the judgement surrounding terms such as 'fussy' or 'picky' eating.

Selective eating as a stage

Selective eating is actually a normal phase that many children go through, and is part of a toddler's development. Between one in five and a third of pre-school children are 'fussy eaters' in one way or another. Choosing what to eat allows a toddler to express their first attempt at independence. It is a small way to take control. Add in the fact that toddlers may need to eat less at certain times, when their growth is slowing, and you can suddenly find yourself with a child who rejects a whole range of foods and only eats half of what you expect. Knowing this is just part of growing up can help you, the parent, stay calm when inside you are worried that your child is going hungry.

A fear of new foods is also natural for children. One theory suggests that it is something that humans developed to protect themselves in the early stages of evolution. Known foods were safe: as a prehistoric toddler learned to walk and explore, knowing to avoid new and unknown foodstuffs would protect them from poisonous plants, for example.

Dr Gillian Harris BA, MSc, PhD is a senior lecturer and consultant clinical psychologist at the Children's Hospital, Birmingham. She explains:

" *The neophobic stage starts around twenty months. Children start to reject food on match of visual prototype. Simply put, this means food has to look the same as it did before. The more sensorily sensitive the child, the more neophobic and anxious they are likely to be. This peaks at about twenty to twenty-four months, and dies down by age five. All children will be neophobic to some degree.* **"**

There are other reasons why toddlers avoid food. Some may be drinking lots of milk, which can leave them feeling full, while others may be filling up on juice or other drinks. A toddler's stomach is relatively small, so drinks or snacks between meals can easily fill them up. Also, while we have heard all the messages about healthy eating, toddlers prefer to eat what they feel like! Many small children seem to almost binge on one food at a time. Ted, aged three, does this, according to his mum, Fiona:

" *Ted could happily just eat sausages one meal, and consume three or four of them. The next day he might only want cucumber. He doesn't eat very consistently at all: one day he might be much hungrier than another.* **"**

This pattern of eating can continue longer than you might expect for children with delayed development or additional needs. Aim to balance your child's meals over the week rather than the day. It meets their needs and makes it easier for you to be relaxed at mealtimes.

Other children may just not be meeting enough new foods, and hence getting no chance to familiarize themselves with different tastes and textures. Children need to see and try some foods several times before accepting them, so ensure that your child gets to try all the foods you might normally eat. Most children who are offered a wide range of foods from weaning are likely to accept them, but only a small percentage of foods are accepted after the age of two. For children with certain conditions this can be more extreme. Keep on offering a range of healthy items, and accept that, for some children, a sniff or a lick might be all they can manage on the first, fifth or even tenth exposure. Delaying introducing different textures can also mean that a child is resistant to eating certain foods.

Laura explains:

" *We moved house when Michael was around nine months old. I didn't think babies would be affected by a house move, but it certainly unsettled him. I admit that I tended to feed him the same baby food in jars around that time: it was just easier when we were all at sixes and sevens. As we got back to normal and I started to cook again it took me a little while to realize that Michael had gone off food that he would have eaten before. He only liked certain types of baby food in jars and would refuse other things. As he got older, this became more of a challenge. The health visitor made a few suggestions when he wouldn't eat anything other than puréed food. We even tried offering him things like Skips, crisps that almost dissolve in your mouth, in order to get him used to different textures. Michael also had bad eczema at that time, and we went through the experience of allergy testing, and it turned out he was allergic to eggs and dairy products.* **"**

When selective eating continues

Beyond these common reasons for selective eating, there are some children who continue to eat a very restricted range of foods well beyond toddlerhood, which can be known as perseverative feeding disorder. There is a lack of detailed information on how selective eating develops, but the Royal College of Psychiatrists (RCP) says that food problems in pre-school children are common. If you are reading this, you are probably one of the group of parents struggling with a child with a limited diet well into primary or secondary school. Dr Gillian Harris explains:

" *I work as a consultant with children with complex feeding difficulties. Children start choosing foods at weaning, and you'll get a difference in acceptance of taste. Children with special needs and sensory hypersensitivity tend to have problems with lumpy solids when introduced at around seven months. Parents* *experience refusal and gagging because a child is trying to do a liquid swallow on a lump. They don't push food round the mouth with their tongue. This is more prevalent with children on the autism spectrum, and in those with Down's syndrome accompanied by sensory hypersensitivity, Russell Silver syndrome, and Turner's syndrome in girls. Children with developmental delay or cleft palate can also show the same difficulties, so you get refusal of lumpy solid textures. Parents back off from offering lumpy food. And if they have not been advised on how to desensitize a child to taste and sensation in the mouth, the child may then go on not to touch finger food. We often see children coming to the clinic in their second year but still on purées. I can do a lot more if a child presents in the first year.* "

Children with continued selective eating issues are often within the normal range for height and weight, according to University College, London's Institute of Child Health. Children in this group can exclude or include 'safe' foods according to food group, colour, texture or even temperature. Some children may only eat cold food, while others may eat no fruit at all, for example. The condition seems to occur more often in boys. In the long term, some children with this condition can experience malnutrition and problems with growth and weight gain.

There are a number of reasons why selective eating can continue, and these can appear together.

Delayed development and sensory issues

If your child has delayed development in any way, this can also affect their eating. Children with conditions such as Down's syndrome may develop control over their tongue movements later, for example. Selective eating can be associated with neurological hard-wiring problems including autism spectrum syndromes, certain types of non-verbal learning disabilities and sensory integration disorders. Children with autism spectrum disorder are more likely to refuse foods and have a more limited food repertoire, according to research. Children with any sort of sensory problem may be hypersensitive to appearance, smell, texture and taste, all of which will make trying new foods a challenge. One theory is that some children have more sensitive taste buds than others. Strong flavours can seem over-whelming to them. Just amongst Antonia's own three children, one has much more of a tolerance for spicy and savoury foods than the other two. Some children with additional needs have a heightened gag or vomit reflex: as a child grows older they can stick to a small range of 'safe' foods to avoid triggering a bad experience.

Dr Harris comments:

" *Those children who are visually hypersensitive start seeing mismatches between everything. They concentrate on local details such as the design on the pot, the writing on a biscuit. This is more common in ASD, and children may refuse to eat food that doesn't match. This goes for food that may have been acceptable before. For example, they used to eat yoghurt, but give a different brand yoghurt in a different style of pot, then all yoghurt will be unacceptable.* "

According to Dr Harris:

" *Disgust starts earlier than we thought – around twenty months – and this also plays a role in children refusing certain foods. Children with an avoidant eating disorder have contamination fears, based on their high sensitivity and high anxiety. This may also show as a refusal to use school toilets. Other expressions might be the belief that if someone touches their food it could be contaminated. Imagine that I hide a jellied eel in your sand-wich or lunchbox – would you ever trust me again? For other children it can be hard to watch others eat with their mouth open or wave food around – imagine a vegetarian trying to eat lunch in a slaughter-yard. That's the same feeling of disgust that these children experience. It can be different for different children: some can't cope with noise, others dislike being watched or shudder at other people's dirty plates. If your child struggles with eating at school they may be better if they start sitting at the very edge of the dining hall. Disgust will tail off a little with exposure.* "

Eleanor's son Andrew has Asperger's syndrome. She explains:

" *Over the years my son has had various difficulties with eating. At some points he was quite food-phobic. Now, though, he is limited in what he'll eat by texture and colour. He won't eat things that are lumpy or sloppy, i.e. anything with a sauce such as bolognese or stew. He doesn't eat veg of any kind or much fruit – because it's 'green'. As a very small child he would choke quite readily on food and could never be left to eat alone, even for a moment. His food preferences started to show when he was about three or four. For a while we were seeing a dietician and experts from the autistic unit about A's eating. These days I try to offer him a variety of foods that I know he can eat and try to introduce as many variations as possible within his parameters, to get as close as possible to a 'normal' diet.*

His primary school was very accommodating about his eating issues. They used to provide special meals for him and let him eat on his own away from the other children. Now, he's nearly thirteen and at high school, he can make his own choices about food. For a while he couldn't eat around other people, but now we can usually find a way to allow him to join in with a social meal. "

Oral defensiveness

Oral defensiveness is one cause for selective eating. While some children are always putting things in their mouths, others dislike anything coming near their mouth, or are defensive towards certain textures, flavours or temperatures. A child with oral defensiveness may persistently fight against having their teeth brushed or their face washed. They may have a limited number of foods that they will eat, or may avoid foods with certain textures. They may try to avoid food making contact with their lips, using only their teeth to take food from their cutlery, and they may gag easily. Oral defensiveness may be accompanied by tactile defensiveness (a dislike of being touched). Children with this condition can dislike messy play and avoid touching food, mud and sand, etc.

Sheila is mum to David, aged five, and Mikey, aged three-and-a-half. While pregnant with David, Sheila suffered from uncontrolled high blood pressure resulting in pre-eclampsia. Delays in the emergency C-section left baby David floppy and unresponsive at birth. He needed ten days' tube feeding in the special care baby unit. Once Sheila took David home she still struggled with his feeding. She says, 'He was never very interested in breastfeeding, unlike his brother.' At nine months, David still seemed to be delayed in his development and Sheila was struggling to wean him. She says, 'We got an appointment at the feeding clinic where I explained how he gagged on even tiny amounts of smooth fruit purées or yoghurts. He wasn't meeting his developmental milestones either.' The dietician changed David over to Fortini at fifteen months. Fortini is a 'complete' milk-based formula food. David continued on this diet, with a bottle for breakfast, one at bedtime and three during the day, but struggles with any other food. By the age of four and a half he had been diagnosed with severe autism and profound learning difficulties. He was referred to a feeding clinic in London, where Sheila met with an occupational therapist, a speech and language therapist, a child psychologist and a paediatrician to decide on which approach to take. She says:

66 *They said that most of his feeding issues are due to sensory processing disorder, which made sense to me. They prescribed messy play with food, things like cream, yoghurt and icing sugar to get him used to different textures. We have to do things like hide toys in cooked pasta. We do this at home, at nursery and in sessions with his OT.* 99

The staff at the feeding clinic indicated that David would be on Fortini for the long term, and progress towards eating was likely to be slow. Sheila says:

66 *We've made progress in the last six months and he now will blow through a straw and even suck a little through a straw. He's really not interested in food, though, and has a very short attention span which means sitting up at the table at mealtime for more than a minute or two is unrealistic. If I bake a cake at*

home he might lick it. He'll try chocolate buttons as they melt in his mouth, and he might lick a crisp, but other dissolving food, like Quavers, haven't been a hit. It is quite stressful. He doesn't get invited to birthday parties, but his brother does. On the odd occasion when he has gone along too, you can see people staring if he is only licking the ketchup off chips, or still drinking milk from a bottle. We've made some progress in that he will now drink juice from a sports bottle. 〃

Emotions, anxiety and OCD

Selective eating can also be linked to obsessive compulsive disorder (OCD) and anxiety disorders. Children with sensory hypersensitivity tend to be anxious. Dr Harris explains:

❝ *Anxiety about change combined with sensory hypersensitivity can become avoidant eating disorder. It is a categorization problem: for most children one biscuit is more or less like another so they will eat all biscuits. To hypersensitive children one biscuit doesn't taste or look like another – this is why you mustn't ever hide anything. Children who are anxious feel they have to stick to the identical food, as any change might not be safe. There was an evolutionary benefit in this as, once mobile, primitive children would only eat food the same as that which their parents gave them. In some children, particularly those on the spectrum, anxiety and hypersensitivity combine to make this basic instinct severely limit acceptable food.* 〃

Children with OCD may have rituals surrounding what food can be eaten, affecting not just their choice of food but how it is prepared, served and eaten.

Some children can continue to use the way they eat as a way to exert control. If refusing foods causes a parent to react in a certain way, the child can repeat the refusal in order to subconsciously manipulate a situation.

Our feelings can affect our appetites. When your child is ill, tired or worried they may feel off their food. Some children can channel external stress inwards, leading to feelings of nausea and food avoidance. Mealtimes can become stressful occurrences in themselves, leading to a cycle of food refusal, heightened emotions and confrontation, increased stress hormones, diminished appetite and anxiety about the next meal.

Life experiences for children with additional needs and health conditions can make eating less straightforward. For example, premature birth and early intubation can delay 'normal' development of eating. If tube feeding continues it can leave the child unconfident or even anxious around food. An aversion to having things in their throat can turn into a food phobia, or a desire to select only foods that seem safe and easy.

Neophobia

Some children can experience neophobia (fear of new things) on its own or in combination with other additional needs. Food neophobia is more likely to occur in children who have had disruption during toddlerhood when they are particularly sensitive to change. For others, neophobia will be related to conditions such as autism.

What to do next

If your child continues to avoid some, or many, foods, seek advice to check on their general health: there are a number of different conditions that can be confused with selective eating so always speak to your general practitioner or your child's paediatrician if you are concerned.

If you have a child who eats selectively, here are some tips. Make sure that you understand why your child avoids food, as that can help you choose the strategies that will work best. Seek professional advice and support to help you.

Relax!

The first thing to do as a parent of a child who eats selectively is to relax! This is easier said than done, but avoiding stressing about mealtimes will improve the situation for you and your child. Research has shown that pressuring children to eat can actually end up with them eating less. Children who are not pressured will eat more.

Eleanor says:

" *When Andrew's eating was at its most difficult, I found it very hard. It felt like he wouldn't eat anything – indeed at one point he would only eat chocolate donuts and drink milk, and only when no one else was there. I had to think quite hard about what feeding my children meant to me and separate that from my son's reality. I also had to relax my ideas about what a nutritious and balanced diet is. When things were at their most extreme I really struggled to feel supported. The National Autistic Society was helpful and they suggested some very good books to read. Food and feeding people is, I think, a complex issue and sometimes it's necessary to work out how much of the awfulness of the situation comes from your own feelings as a mother and how much from what actually is going on. If your child has particular difficulties, then don't use normal measures to judge what's happening – for some children five-a-day is an impossible dream and simply getting enough calories in is a battle.* "

She advises other parents, 'The worst of it will pass and it's crucial to relax. Your own stress will transfer to your child and kill whatever little appetite they have.'

Relaxation is key for children too. Dr Harris says, 'Relaxation is an important part of treating sensory hypersensitivity because of the anxiety associated with the condition. We teach the child deep muscle relaxation so they can calm themselves down. The more anxious you are the more hyper-vigilant you are, which for a child with avoidant food disorder means they reject food.'

Alongside taking the pressure off, you can sometimes find that distraction helps your child finish what's on their plate. Different things will work for different children: some hate noise at mealtimes, while others will find that their attention is drawn by music, for example, and they then eat without noticing. Other positive distractions could include telling a story, reading a poem, or looking at pictures or a toy. Dr Harris uses these techniques with patients:

" *If you need practical tips to help a child who struggles with the social aspect of eating and has limited acceptable foods, you need to relax some of the rules you may have. Let the child sit in another room if they don't like eating with others. Use the television or iPad as a distraction, which reduces anxiety in children with special needs. This doesn't work in the same way for a normally developing child, so I wouldn't advise it except in this context. Make it contingent: put a video on, and as long as the child is eating the video is on. One mum I know uses an iPad: the child can have the iPad at mealtimes, but only while eating. They don't let him use the iPad at other times, and if he isn't eating it goes away. Be wary of using certain sorts of reward, such as 'You'll get pudding if you eat your vegetables.' Sometimes what happens if you are not careful is that it you can devalue the instrumental task (the vegetables in this case). Instead, pair something nice with the less pleasant task.* "

Eating is more fun with friends. Invite friend's kids over who eat well, and have family mealtimes where your child can see you eating a healthy variety of food.

Lead by example as most children will copy their parents to a greater or lesser extent. If you mainly eat chips and chocolate, your child will think that is a normal healthy diet.

Explore the issues of refusing food together in an age-appropriate way. For example, you might like to share books like *I Will Not Ever Never Eat a Tomato*, a tale about Charlie and Lola by Lauren Child, or *Night of the Veggie Monster* by George McClements, about a small boy and his battle with three peas! Your child might be reassured by these stories of other children who dislike certain foods. The positive messages can reassure you both – watch out for the slightly sarcastic parents in the Veggie Monster book.

Have a set time for meals of, say, twenty minutes: adapt this to your child and your family's needs. Sitting at a table in front of a plate of cooling food can be stressful for everyone. At the end of the set time, take the food away without a fuss. Children will learn that they need to eat within a set time.

Make meals count

As a parent, it is nearly impossible to avoid worrying if your child does not eat. Reassure yourself that most children will not starve themselves, and appetites can vary from day to day. Monitor your child's snacks and drinks – snacks close to mealtimes can stop your child eating the main meal, and kids with small stomachs can easily fill up on drinks rather than food. Share your concerns with a health practitioner, and they can help you ensure that your child is not losing weight.

Some children with limited diets may be at risk of health problems. Anaemia, for example, is caused by lack of iron in the diet, so do your best within the limits of your child's diet. If your child only eats peas and no other vegetables, that's a start as they are consuming one vegetable.

Dr Harris advises:

“ *If you are worried about your child's weight, again, you may need to discard some rules that apply to the general population. If your child is falling off the line on their growth chart, I'll ask 'Are you giving enough of the child's preferred food?' Parents are trying to give food they think the child should eat. In my clinic we don't have junk food – we have 'calorie-dense' food. With a normally developing child, you might say, 'No' to chocolate, but it is a good source of iron for a child with a very limited range of acceptable foods, so give them that. Whether they want pain au chocolat or fromage frais or a sausage for breakfast – let them! If your child is losing weight, make sure they eat calorie-dense food every two hours. If the school says your child can't have chocolate at mid-morning break, yet it is the only thing they will eat, get a letter from their doctor.* **”**

If you need to offer foods with high nutritional value, ideas for nutrient-dense healthy foods include:

✓ Avocados
✓ Pasta
✓ Broccoli

✓ Peanut butter
✓ Potatoes
✓ Cheese
✓ Poultry
✓ Eggs
✓ Squash
✓ Fish
✓ Sweet potatoes
✓ Beans and pulses
✓ Tofu
✓ Yoghurt

Which foods on this list might appeal to your child? Bring out the highly nutritious foods at the start of a meal when your child is most hungry. Offer more challenging food when your child is hungry, but not tired! Don't try new foods if you are in a hurry. Watch out for 'kids foods': if you only offer your child fish fingers, smiley potato faces or chicken nuggets, they will struggle when faced with more 'adult' food.

Dr Harris advises that you need to be cautious before you risk boosting your child's calorific intake by hiding foods: 'At this stage, hiding food is the worst thing you can do. Mixed up foods may not look the same to your child. For example, we had a paediatrician advising a parent whose child would always eat Ready brek to hide puréed apple in it. The child stopped eating Ready brek'.

Eat your peas

If you have a child over five who is eating a very narrow range of food, this is called an avoidant diet. Keep things consistent. If you want to expand what they will eat, introduce a new food that looks very similar to an acceptable food.

As an example, if your child only likes peas, give them more than one vegetable to choose from at mealtimes, for example, by offering peas *and* broad beans or sweetcorn, and let them see other people eating both of the offered vegetables. Don't make a big fuss about the new vegetable. Keep the language you use neutral, rather than saying 'I don't expect Tim will eat this' or even 'How exciting, it's carrots!'

Just bring out the vegetables without comment. Offer a plate of vegetable, fruit and cheese pieces as a healthy snack, or a range of chopped vegetables and dips if you want to expand the range of vegetables that your child eats. Separate food if that is what your child prefers, allowing them to pick the food they like, and become more familiar with new foods. A sniff, touch or lick of a new item of food can be considered a win! Remember that your child may need to see the food many times before deciding it is acceptable.

If your child is younger, Dr Harris suggests:

" *Prior to the neophobic stage, make sure you offer your child plenty of different foods. For example, don't always buy the same biscuits. If you always buy one brand your child may stick with only accepting that brand. We're very consistent in our purchasing behaviour. Present a biscuit that's from a different shop* before *the neophobic stage to ensure that several different brands of biscuit are acceptable. If your child eats yoghurt, make sure that you offer a range of yoghurts before this stage.* **"**

I won't eat meat

Meat can be another area of conflict, and older children may actively decide to be vegetarian. If your younger child doesn't eat meat, however, you may want to encourage them. Meat can be hard for children to chew. Cut it into small pieces, and cut across the grain to minimize the chewing your child will have to do. Casseroling meat can make it tender: Antonia has cooked meat in this way then scraped off the sauce for the non-sauce eaters in the family. Minced meat, sausages and burgers can be more acceptable to children: pick the best quality ones that you can afford as these tend to have a higher meat content, more nutrients and less fat. For children who won't eat meat, offer a range of foods such as fish, eggs, nuts and pulses. Pulses include chickpeas and lentils. These include protein that will help your child stay healthy, as do beans.

The texture challenge

For some children who are orally defensive, the challenge of new food is about the texture or temperature just as much as the taste. Consider whether your child only likes cold food, for example, or will only eat purées, or hates sloppy food.

If this sounds like the situation you are facing, you'll find it more acceptable to introduce new foods that are similar to what your child tolerates already. In the longer term, however, you want to introduce hot, cold and warm foods. For children who have issues with textures, move from purées to thicker smooth foods, to food with lumps. If your child likes 'dry' food, think about how you can gradually get them to accept sticky or slippery foods. Just attempt one change at a time. Understanding this approach can help you succeed in widening your child's repertoire and pick new foods that are close in texture or temperature to those that they accept already.

More ideas for hypersensitive children

Dr Harris regularly works with children who have sensory hypersensitivity. She says:

&& *To help children who are hypersensitive, we get the occupational therapist involved. An OT can advise on a desensitization programme of massage and messy play to help the child increase their acceptance of touch. A specialist speech and language therapist can also advise on desensitizing the inside of the mouth with age-appropriate activities. In a young baby this could simply be massaging gums with a finger. Some children will be hypersensitive to taste, some to texture, some to messy hands – all of these link back to hypersensitivity, with tactile hypersensitivity playing the most important role, followed by smell and taste.* &&

If your child just doesn't like putting things in or near their mouths, here are a few more ideas to help them desensitize:

✓ Rub your child's cheeks with different textured soft cloths
✓ Experiment with different toothbrushes. Try a vibrating toothbrush, which gets your child used to a different sensation in their mouth

✓ Offer a small ice lolly before meals to help desensitize their mouth
✓ Ask for referral to an occupational therapist (OT) or speech and language therapist (SLT) – see Chapter 12
✓ The OT/SLT may suggest an oral massager, finger toothbrush or 'chewy tubes' to help your child get used to sensations near their mouth

These suggestions should be carried out with the supervision of a therapist. Sheila has had various helpful suggestions from her son's SLT. She says:

" *We were recommended to use a vibrating toothbrush to get him used to different sensations near his mouth. That was successful, he really likes it and likes cleaning his teeth. We have a vibrating toy snake, which he likes holding against his face and mouth. He is very sensitive still to temperature. He'll screw up his face if we offer him an ice lolly, and flinches away from anything hot.* **"**

Rewarding your child

Some children are just not interested in food. They stick to a range of preferred foods and see no reason to change. If your child does not want to try new foods, think what might motivate them. Depending on their ability and interest, devise a reward chart. Give a sticker each time they try something new. Seven attempts at trying something new might lead to a small reward. Adding something new to the list of 'things I will eat' could mean a bigger reward.

Beyond rewards, always praise your child for trying something new. Remember, you can praise them for a sniff or a lick: this is all part of broadening their experience of food, the first step to eating a greater range of items.

Dr Harris creates programmes to help children try new foods. She advises:

" *Children with autism may eat different foods in different contexts: for example, your child may eat certain foods at school as they like the TA who helps them at mealtimes.*

Children with Asperger's tend to eat the same food everywhere. We wait until they are a little older – past the age of eight – before we move them on to try new foods. We create a taste programme to help children experience new foods. It starts with relaxation, and then, away from mealtimes, they try something new. It helps to allow the child choice so they are motivated to try new things. Offer them their choice of reward – I find boys are often motivated by time on the computer. For older boys it might simply be that they want to be able to share pizza with their friends: that is enough motivation to try it. ""

Family meals

It is best to offer one meal for the whole family. Try to avoid the trap of different meals for different family members, or even worse, making a fresh meal if the first one is rejected. You might want to start with a list of a few meals that are acceptable to most of the family, and repeat those every week to build familiarity. If your child only eats chocolate spread sandwiches and hates food in sauces, and you are serving the family macaroni cheese, include a tiny portion of plain macaroni on their plate as a start. Nell says, 'There's something to be said for family meals. Jake will eat food from my plate that he wouldn't try if I put it straight on his plate. We were surprised that he liked Indian food: we didn't start off offering it to him, but he wanted to try it.'

Drinkwise

It is easy for your child to fill up on drinks. If you are concerned that your child isn't eating enough, monitor their liquid intake between meals. Offer water rather than milk or juice, and make sure your child eats food before drinking. Sometimes your child may continue to want a bottle for longer than you had expected. A bottle can be used for comfort sucking by children, leading to a greater intake of milk than your child might need. If your child finds their bottle comforting, consider replacing milk with water as a first step to lessening their need for it. Talk to your health visitor for advice.

Supplements

For a child with limited appetite who eats a small range of foods or who is failing to grow properly or thrive, your community dietician may advise vitamin and mineral drops. A, C and D are commonly given to small children.

Siblings

Sometimes your child's selective eating habits can spread within the family! Eleanor says:

" Richard is now ten, two-and-a-half years younger than Andrew. Because Andrew was so difficult to feed Richard didn't have to try new food and often ate the same bland dry 'kid food' as his brother. By the time I realized what was going on he was totally picky and won't try new food. He also adopted a lot of his brother's weirdnesses such as refusing to eat the ends of sausages or broken foods. "

If this sounds like your situation, make sure that the whole family eats together, so siblings can learn from different people's eating habits. Problems can go beyond simply eating too. Sheila says:

" It is difficult for Mikey as he sees that we have two sets of rules. He has to sit at the table, eat his meal and then ask to get down. His older brother, in contrast, doesn't eat any food, wanders away from the table, and only drinks his special formula. Mikey says that he wants milk too. Mikey has seen his brother struggling to do painful bowel movements and has started withholding his own movements. "

Sheila says, 'I heard him tell a friend, "I don't poo".' We've had to go to the GP for senna to help him go, and I'm going to have to talk to the constipation nurse specialist about him too. I'm hoping it will help at pre-school where he sees other children going to the toilet without problems.

See www.sibs.org.uk, an organization for brothers and sisters of disabled children and adults, for more ideas to help the family.

Cooking and gardening

Get your child involved in all parts of a meal – from simply putting their own plate on the table to growing vegetables.

Preparing food can be fun, even for children who don't think they'll like the finished result! Learning about what goes into food can encourage your child to take a tiny taste as they help with the cooking. Even licking their fingers after cooking, though it might seem unhygienic, can introduce them to new flavours. There is a certain amount of pride in being able to tell the family that you helped make a meal, and this can give your child positive feelings around food to replace some of their more negative ideas.

If your child can share their views, get them involved in meal planning for everyone. Deciding whether it is lamb or chicken for dinner can make them feel good. A shopping trip to choose food for dinner for everyone can also help. There is no need to offer unlimited choices: say something like 'Which pasta will we cook today – long ones or short ones?'

If you're not a gardener, or have limited space, an old bucket with a few holes for drainage is the perfect place to grow a potato. Don't panic about getting 'special' potatoes to grow – use a leftover one from the bottom of the fridge! Visiting a pick-your-own farm can also help your child learn about food and where it comes from. And there are a number of children's cooking programmes that also show where food comes from and how to make a meal.

Read more about getting your child involved in food activities in Chapter 8.

In summary

If you have a selective eater, it can seem as though you are standing at the bottom of a steep mountain as you consider how to get them to eat a healthy diet. Remember that you are not alone. Seek professional advice if you feel that you need extra support with your child's eating to help them grow healthily.

Take each day at a time. Pick the best time to give your child a new or challenging food: don't feel that you have to try something new every mealtime. Work round their preferences, set a time to stay at the table during mealtimes, and then end the meal before it becomes a battlefield. Ideally, have family meals as much as possible, so your child can see how other people eat. You will soon discover what works best for you and your child.

Sally's son has Asperger's, which means he is quite clear about what is and isn't acceptable when he eats. She explains that he 'has to have his food laid out, not wet (with gravy/sauce) and he doesn't like things mixed up'. Tom's issues began when he was around five years old, and Sally has adapted. She says: 'We tend to dish up his food now with large gaps in between each item, so they don't touch. It was a bit of a pain in the beginning but now I have got used to managing it. We tend to test food with him so that we do not dish up something he does not like.'

Sally advises other parents, 'My biggest tip would be to cook small bits of "strange food" and let them try it before you actually put it on their plates. For me dishing up an item that he has never had before is setting him up for 'blow-up'/tantrum.'

Dr Harris sums up by saying:

❝ *My top tips: Never force feed your child; don't hide or disguise food. Act as a great role model for your child. Show them how you eat new foods and they are more likely to try them. For some children stickers will work as a reward. For others, they may be rewarded by one-to-one interaction as you try the food or sit with them while they eat.* ❞

Read more strategies for helping your child cope with food in chapters 8, 9 and 10.

Chapter 5
Food and Emotions

Food and emotions are closely linked. Eating can help to deal with emotions and also create emotion. Children quickly learn that food can be used as a source of comfort, as a child may be given a piece of cake to cheer them up. Children may also learn that food is used as a reward: sweets or chocolate may be given to congratulate a child on achieving tasks. This kind of behaviour continues into adulthood. Think about the times when you've eaten a piece of birthday cake just to be sociable, or poured yourself a glass of wine as a reward for completing a challenging task or simply getting to the end of another day.

Some children have negative emotions associated with food and eating. A child may, for example, have anxiety around choking or a fear of trying new foods. Eating disorders involve negative emotions about body weight and food and are another area that we will explore in this chapter.

Your emotions and food

Children will pick up on your emotions around food and mealtimes. If you are worried and anxious around mealtimes they will realize and this may feed their negative emotions. Kate Barlow is a Parent Consultant at www.parentconsultancy.com. Kate tells us:

" *Many parents worry that their child is not eating or drinking enough. Children's appetite for food and drink will vary from day to day and will depend on how much physical activity they are getting and the stage of development. The best advice you can follow is to relax and not make mealtimes a big issue. By offering your child a wide variety of food and respecting their appetite you will encourage good eating habits. Healthy children will not starve themselves and they can survive on few calories and often make up for it in time when their appetite increases.* "

Dr Pippa Rundle says:

" *Children usually pick up anxiety from the caring adults, and very quickly learn which eating behaviours cause most alarm. This might be throwing food, refusing to eat, or just eating very slowly. All of these behaviours draw attention to the child and with constant cajoling and offering alternative foods, the meal can last up to an hour. The more anxious the parent becomes, the more the behaviour is repeated.*

Parents are usually most anxious when their child has been very small at birth, and gaining weight is an important issue. The situation can become tense and spoil the pleasure of eating. "

It is therefore very important to keep your own emotions in check at mealtimes so that you do not pass on your anxiety.

Here are some tips to help:

✓ Concentrate on your breathing. If you are feeling anxious take long, slow deep breaths
✓ Remember that the situation will pass and don't blow it out of all proportion
✓ Ask for some help if there is somebody who can take over from you for a few moments
✓ If safe to do, so leave the room to gather your composure
✓ Focus on the positives rather than the negatives

Sheila's son has autism and eating issues. She says:

" *We get support from the Family Intensive Support service. I have a lady who visits me every couple of weeks, and a child psychologist comes to help with advice about the boys' behaviour every six weeks or so. It is good to have someone to consult: we had problems when David was in lots of discom-*

fort and lashing out at his brother. The child psychologist gives me advice on how to break the cycle. I also have the benefit of someone to talk to, someone who will help chase things up, or find out where we can access support or services that we need. She helped us create a book of images so David could point to what he wanted to do, and make choices between milk or juice, for example. 〞

Food aversion

Some children develop an aversion to specific types of food. This can trigger a response which may make them become extremely anxious if presented with that type of food and in some cases they may even be sick. Food aversions can develop because of things that have happened in the past. For example, Gilli is seven years old and has an aversion to sandwiches irrespective of what the filling contains. Her mum says:

〝 *When Gilli was three years old she was sick while eating a cheese sandwich. From that day on she developed a strong aversion to sandwiches. If she sees a sandwich she can begin to gag. I've tried to present sandwiches in different shapes and sizes, changing the filling and so on but nothing seems to work.* 〞

Aversions like this can be extremely strong and may last a lifetime. Some children benefit from watching others eating the item or from desensitization by way of handling the food and smelling it. If a child has a food aversion you should not force them to eat the food as this can escalate the problem – seek advice from a health practitioner.

Fear of choking or swallowing

Some children have a fear of choking; this is called pseudodysphagia. Anxiety can cause the throat muscles to constrict, which can then actually increase the risk of choking. Some children may refuse to eat solid foods because of this fear. Sometimes children develop a fear of choking after they have had an incident of choking on food. Usually this will quickly resolve itself. If your child has a fear of choking it is important to seek medical advice as soon as possible. Don't try to force your child to eat solid food; this may lead to further distress and anxiety.

Phagophobia is the name for the fear of swallowing. This can again be caused through anxiety and psychological treatment is required, which can include cognitive behavioural therapy techniques. Relaxation techniques can also be helpful and will be explored later in this chapter.

Anger and eating issues

Research suggests that there is a direct link between anger and eating disorders. Anger can be a useful emotion but if your child's anger becomes out of control it can impact on all aspects of their life, including their eating. Children with additional needs may need support in order to manage these difficult feelings in a positive way. It can be helpful to try to work out what the triggers for your child's anger may be. Make a note of times when they do become angry and try to establish what might have caused this. Triggers may be things like tiredness, hunger or frustration. When you are aware of the triggers you can become more able to intervene before the anger escalates. It is important that your child has a way of managing their anger. Some children need to be provided with a quiet space to retreat to when they are feeling angry.

Emotional eating

Emotional eating is when food is used to deal with feelings rather than to suppress hunger. Emotional eating can impact on your child's weight and health. We usually associate negative emotions with emotional eating, for example, we may eat when we are:

✓ Depressed
✓ Bored
✓ Anxious
✓ Lonely
✓ Sad

Emotional eating can, however, also be linked to positive emotions. For example, we may eat when we are:

✓ Celebrating an event such as a birthday or Christmas
✓ Happy
✓ Sharing with a friend
✓ Being rewarded

Emotional eating can be learned from a parent. It is important, therefore, that you have a healthy attitude towards food. A child who is rewarded with chocolate may learn to reward themselves with food. Or if you give a child a biscuit to 'cheer them up', they may learn to eat biscuits to gain comfort. Avoid using food as a reward or a comfort.

Managing anxiety

If your child is anxious it may impact not only on their eating but also on their daily functioning. If the anxiety is ongoing and severe you may need to seek professional advice. Initially, speak to your child's health care provider in order to share your concerns.

There are strategies that you can adopt at home to help your child to manage their anxiety levels. Here are some tips to follow:

✓ Acknowledge your child's anxieties rather than dismissing them and give them the opportunity to share their feelings
✓ Offer distractions if appropriate so that they don't become immersed in their anxiety issues
✓ Establish routines; these help children to feel more secure
✓ Be aware of your own anxieties and make a conscious effort not to pass these on
✓ Create a calm home environment
✓ Make sure that your child gets enough sleep; there is a direct link between sleep deprivation and anxiety

Emotions can be extremely confusing and children with additional needs may require support to understand feelings. There are a number of excellent books on the market that explain about feelings: many of these are aimed specifically at children with additional needs (see Chapter 12 for examples). Your child may benefit from having some emotion cards which show different feelings pictorially. When they are happy you should give them the appropriate card and tell them 'you are feeling happy'. This will help them to make sense of their emotions in a positive manner.

Relaxation is important for children; sometimes they need to be taught techniques in order to reduce their anxiety levels and promote relaxation. There are a number of strategies that you can adopt to help your child to relax. These include:

✓ Listening to relaxation CDs, see Chapter 12 for resources
✓ Carrying out breathing exercises to help them to calm down. Get them to imagine that they are blowing up a big balloon. The outward breath should be longer than the inward breath
✓ Listening to classical music, which can be very calming
✓ Receiving a massage
✓ Guided imagery. Put on some nice music and talk your child through an imaginary journey that you know they will enjoy, for example, a trip to the seaside. Focus on listening to the waves, feeling the sun on their face and so on. There are some books produced with scripts that are helpful, see Chapter 12 for ideas
✓ Reading stories that deal with emotions such as worry and anger; titles are included in Chapter 12

Eating disorders

Many youngsters become concerned about how they look, particularly during the teenage years. For some this can lead them to becoming obsessed with food and lead to eating disorders such as anorexia nervosa or bulimia nervosa. Both of these conditions can have a serious impact on health and well-being.

Parents play an important role in helping to prevent eating disorders. It is important to build your child's self-esteem and to encourage a healthy outlook about appearance and weight. If you suspect that your child has an eating disorder you should seek medical advice as soon as possible.

Signs that indicate that your child may have an eating disorder include:

✓ Weight loss or fluctuation
✓ Obsession with food and weight control
✓ Excessive exercising
✓ Change of eating habits, for example, limiting food or not taking part in celebrations involving food
✓ Low self-esteem about their appearance

Anorexia nervosa

Anorexia leads sufferers to have a fear of gaining weight. They have a distorted view of their body's size and shape. Sufferers restrict their food intake in order to maintain a low weight. They may exercise excessively, diet or not eat at all. They become obsessed by calorific intake and obsess about the food that they eat. People with anorexia become very underweight; the body goes into starvation mode, which can lead to a number of physical symptoms including:

✓ Loss of hair
✓ Lowered blood pressure
✓ Weak fingernails
✓ Anaemia
✓ Brittle bones

Bulimia nervosa

People with bulimia will binge on food and their weight may fluctuate though they rarely become very underweight. In fact some people with bulimia may even be overweight. Again there may be compulsive exercising, vomiting or use of laxatives. Bulimia involves regular vomiting and the body becomes starved of nutrients leading to a number of symptoms. These may include:

✓ Stomach pains
✓ Damage to the kidneys

✓ Disruption to the menstrual cycle
✓ Damaging of teeth caused by erosion from stomach acid
✓ Mineral deficiency

Help for eating disorders

The cause of eating disorders is not known though it is likely that it involves a range of issues such as genetic, social and psychological factors. Children with anxiety disorders and obsessive compulsive disorder (OCD) are more at risk of developing an eating disorder. Some children may develop an eating disorder as a way of maintaining some control in their lives. If you suspect that your child has an eating disorder it is important to seek professional help. Treatment can help with establishing new thought patterns around food.

In summary

There is a direct link between emotions and eating. It is important that your child is taught about emotions in a way that will help them make sense of their feelings. It is also vital that your child learns relaxation techniques. As a parent you are an important role model for your child's eating habits. You therefore need to be aware of this and have a positive attitude about food. Parent consultant Kate Barlow believes that parents provide an important role model around eating. She says:

" *Lead by example and enjoy mealtimes with your child; eat the same foods as your child as much as possible. Food manufactured especially for children is a relatively new phenomenon. Children will eat and should eat the same foods as adults, but in smaller portions; they are much more likely to do so if they see you enjoying yours.* "

Chapter 6
Food, Diet and Eating Issues Relating to Specific Conditions

If your child has a diagnosis of a specific special need you may find that eating issues can be linked to their condition. In this chapter we will be exploring different eating issues that are commonly found in children who have been diagnosed with special needs. While all children are individuals irrespective of their additional needs, some conditions do have more direct links to eating and food issues.

Global developmental delay

Global developmental delay is a term used to describe a situation when a child has a delay in two or more areas. Children who are developmentally delayed may find that their feeding skills are also delayed. They may teethe later than other babies, which can hinder the chewing process. If you are worried about your child's teeth or lack of them you should speak to your dentist. It can be helpful to massage gums and it is important to still introduce a tooth-brushing routine so that your child accepts having their teeth cleaned as routine.

Motor skills can be affected by developmental delay, which can mean that children find it more difficult to feed themselves. It is important to remain patient with your child and to concentrate on what they can achieve rather than focusing on what they haven't yet mastered. Children learn a great deal from seeing positive role models. Make sure that you eat with your child so that they can see how to behave at mealtimes. Give your child lots of praise for making attempts at self-feeding even if it is messy! If you are concerned about their feeding you should seek advice from a medical professional.

Down's syndrome

If you have a child who has Down's syndrome you may find that their eating is also affected. If you have a baby with Down's syndrome you may find that they grow slowly; there are special weight and height charts produced for children by the Down's Syndrome Medical Interest Group. You can contact them by logging on to www.dsmig.org.uk. The group is aimed at health care professionals but it is useful to know about them in order to make professionals that are involved in your child's care aware of the information available.

Feeding difficulties may be experienced from birth if your child has low muscle tone. If you are worried about how much milk your baby is taking you should discuss this with your health visitor. Children with Down's syndrome can take longer than their peers to learn how to chew and swallow, which means that weaning may take more time. They may also show a preference for smoother foods as opposed to more textured meals. If you are unsure about your child's weaning you should approach your health visitor for support; the key thing to keep in mind is that you want to offer your child a healthy diet.

It is important that you do seek advice if you feel that there is a feeding problem. The muscles used to chew are going to be important later on when it comes to learning to speak. Sometimes children need to be referred to a speech and language therapist for support with feeding issues.

Some children with Down's syndrome suffer with bowel abnormalities that can vary in how they impact on a child's eating. Often these are diagnosed prior to birth or very quickly after birth. Your child may be more prone to being constipated or having diarrhoea; they may also suffer from gastro-oesophageal reflux. If you notice any of these signs you should speak to your paediatrician as they may indicate a bowel problem. See Chapter 3 for more about these specific conditions.

It is very common for children with Down's syndrome to have constipation. This can be because they are not as mobile as other children, or not drinking enough. Sometimes children need to be prescribed a laxative to help with the issue. It is important that you give your child lots of drinks during the day and also make sure that they are eating enough fruit and fibre within their diet. Any change in bowel habit should be noted and discussed with the paediatrician. Sometimes a chronically constipated child can suffer with diarrhoea if their back passage becomes blocked; there can be an overflow effect. There is more about constipation and diarrhoea in Chapter 3.

Coeliac disease is also more common in children with Down's syndrome. This is when there is an inability to digest food containing gluten. Gluten is found in wheat products. If you think that your child may have an intolerance to wheat discuss this with your paediatrician before making changes to your child's diet.

Autism spectrum disorders

Children with autism spectrum disorders may also have eating difficulties. 'Autism spectrum disorders' is an umbrella term for a wide range of disorders. Not all children who have an autism spectrum disorder will have food issues and not all food issues will be the same. Eating issues are, however, extremely common in children on the autism spectrum and can present themselves in a number of ways. Some children will only eat certain foods, or foods of one consistency or texture. Because children with autism are likely to have sensory hypersensitivity, foods that seem much the same to us can appear unacceptably different to them. This can be accompanied by a higher level of anxiety which can affect eating too. See Chapter 4 for more about sensory hypersensitivity and anxiety, and Chapter 5 for more about our emotions and how they affect how we eat.

Jayne has a son with Asperger's syndrome and tells us:

" *Alfie's diet is quite limited; he is unwilling to try anything new. He likes to eat pasta but won't tolerate any sauce on it. He will also only eat one brand of pasta even though to me they all taste the same. This started really when he was about two-and-a-half years old; up until then he would try most foods.* "

Some children can also be highly sensitive to the smells of different foods. Angie has a daughter who is on the autism spectrum and she tells us:

" *Eliza refuses to try new foods and will only eat a certain brand of cheesy pasta. She is very sensitive to taste and smells of foods and this started when she was a toddler. The doctor has provided us with food supplements in the form of vitamins. She takes a packed lunch to school but we can't go out as a family to eat socially any longer. Initially I felt like a failure until I realized that I was not to blame. I still keep introducing new foods to her in the hope that one day she will try something else. It's a very slow process but I'd say to other parents just persevere, don't give up, just because they won't eat something this week doesn't mean they won't try it next week.* "

Some children on the autism spectrum find that mealtimes are too noisy if they are dining with others. Using ear defenders can help with this problem. Jill has a son who is twelve years old and has an autism spectrum disorder. She tells us:

" *Jon can sometimes be fine when we eat out yet on other occasions he can become distressed and can't tolerate the noise. He will frequently cover his ears and ask to use the toilet to get out of the environment. Recently on one occasion he became very distressed and started to cry. It makes eating out very stressful. I've bought him an iPod with headphones and I've found this to be a helpful strategy. He will now listen to this if in an environment that he finds too loud and it seems to help him to calm down and tolerate the background noise better.* "

Sitting to eat at mealtimes can put social pressure on a child with autism. It may be that you need to gradually build up the amount of time for which your child can sit at the dinner table. Sand timers are a useful resource as a child can see how long they must remain seated before leaving the table. You can purchase sand timers in various units of time and gradually extend the length of time for which your child is expected to sit at the table.

Attention Deficit Hyperactivity Disorder (ADHD)

If your child has a diagnosis of ADHD you may find that they are underweight and you may worry about their food intake. Children with ADHD are extremely active and can burn off calories more quickly than their peers. They can also find mealtimes challenging as they can find it hard to remain seated for sustained periods of time in order to eat meals. Medication associated with ADHD can also reduce a child's appetite; ask your paediatrician about possible side effects of any medication.

Children with ADHD may not take in adequate liquids, meaning that they dehydrate or that when they do sit down to eat a meal they immediately fill up on liquids rather than on food. It can be helpful to prompt your child to drink an hour or so before mealtimes to ensure that they do take in adequate fluids throughout the day. Milkshakes are a useful and fun way of getting additional calories into reluctant eaters.

Cerebral palsy

Some children with cerebral palsy may also have feeding issues. Difficulties can range from mild to more severe. Feeding issues may become apparent from birth and numerous professionals may become involved in order to offer guidance and management around your child's feeding issues.

Physiotherapists will identify the best position for your child, as positioning is very important during eating. A speech and language therapist may be required to assess and offer advice around your child's eating. They will be able to offer you guidance about how to encourage your child to develop their chewing pattern and, if you feed your child, where to place the food in their mouth. Some children with cerebral palsy have difficulty keeping their mouths closed whilst eating and others may push the food out of their mouth with their tongue. Some children may also have difficulties with their gag reflex, which means they can find it difficult to cough and stop food from going down the wrong way. Advice around gag reflexes should be sought from a speech therapist or your child's paediatrician.

An occupational therapist will be able to assess your child for any specialist equipment that is required. This can include items such as specialist cutlery: more information about these sorts of items is included in Chapter 12 of this book. A dietician may also be involved to offer advice around nutrition and to support you to ensure that your child's diet remains healthy.

Rebecca has a daughter who has feeding issues and cerebral palsy. She tells us:

" *There are lots of different professionals involved in Heather's care. I've found that a 'Team Around the Child' approach works best in managing her care. We have a meeting around once every six weeks where the professionals involved get together with ourselves. We discuss how she has been getting on, any issues, what our priorities are for the future. It is really useful as she has a physiotherapist, occupational therapist, dietician and speech therapist all involved with her feeding. They can discuss ideas while we are there and they all bring their own area of expertise to the table. It makes it far easier than having to take her to the different therapists individually. If you have a child with feeding issues and a number of professionals involved I would ask if you can use this approach to make dealing with the issues more manageable for you as a family.* **"**

Sensory issues can also affect children with cerebral palsy. Some children can find they are hypersensitive around their faces; this can cause them to pull away when being fed. Oral tactile defensiveness is the term that is used to describe oversensitivity around being touched near the mouth and is covered in Chapter 4. Sometimes children may reject food with different textures, for example, sponge and custard. Other children may be unaware of touch around their mouth; this means that they may be unaware of food being in their mouth or of the fact that they are drooling.

There are programmes that can be used in order to desensitize or help to sensitize children to touch around their mouth. You should seek advice from your speech therapist or occupational therapist around how to use different foods to increase your child's tolerance to touch/different textures.

Pica

Pica is an eating disorder where individuals eat non-food items such as sand, soft furnishings or even hair. At some point most children will put non-food items into their mouth to explore them; youngsters with pica, however, will consistently eat non-food items. If you have noticed that your child eats non-food items you should speak to your GP in the first instance. You should be concerned if your child consumes non-food items for four weeks or longer.

Pica occurs most commonly in youngsters with learning disabilities and autism spectrum disorders. Pica can develop in those who have suffered a brain injury, those with epilepsy and also in pregnant women. Those who have pica will crave non-food items and some of the items eaten can lead to serious health issues.

It is not fully known why pica occurs but some theories suggest that it can be caused by nutritional deficiencies, which can trigger a craving. The food craved, however, often doesn't supply the lacking nutrient. Developmental disorders can lead to pica as can mental health disorders such as obsessive compulsive disorder (OCD) or bipolar.

You should seek urgent medical attention if you believe that your child may have eaten something potentially harmful or poisonous. Pica can cause health issues such as bowel problems if your child eats substances that cannot be digested, such as hair. Your child may also be at risk of objects becoming lodged in the intestines or causing perforation. Some objects that children eat can cause dental injury and others may cause infection, for example, if your child eats faeces. There is no diagnostic test for pica but behavioural approaches can be employed to help you and your child to manage pica more effectively. Medication can at times be prescribed if your child does not respond to behavioural approaches to tackling the problem. It is a good idea to have your child checked out for nutritional deficiencies if they have pica. It is usually a short-term condition, however, it can persist with children who have additional needs.

Visual impairments

For a child with a visual impairment it is important that their other senses are used during mealtimes. They may need time to smell their food before eating it. If they have good understanding then you may need to provide them with a commentary about what is on their plate so that they know what to expect to taste next. Depending on your child's age and level of understanding you could describe the different foods and their position using a clock, e.g., 'Your potato is at nine o'clock, your meat is at two o'clock and the carrots are at six o'clock'. Some children are able to see better when food is presented on a different coloured background: mashed potato is much harder to see on a white plate, and easier to see on a coloured plate. You may need to experiment to see if the colour of the plate makes any difference to their ability to see what is on the plate in front of them and also experiment with the positioning of the plate. If you feed your child they should be forewarned that the food is about to be tasted and the first taste should be small so that they can see if they like it or not.

Gemma has a son with a visual impairment and tells us:

I attended a brilliant training course about eating and visual impairments. We were blindfolded and fed different tastes, textures and so on. It really made me think about how I feed my son. It was horrible when too much was fed to me too quickly and I hadn't a clue about what might be coming next, which left me feeling very vulnerable. I now make sure that I communicate fully with Max when I feed him and let him know what he's about to taste. I also look for signs that he is ready to experience the next mouthful rather than just spooning it in.

Hearing impairments

If your child has a hearing impairment and requires you to feed them you should ensure that they can see what food is on the plate. Take time to show them the food and to let them know what they are about to eat. Also ensure that they have seen the food on the spoon approaching their mouth so that they don't become startled. Your child may need to be given time to touch and smell the food prior to eating it too.

Tube feeding

Sometimes it is necessary for a child to be tube fed. Tube feeding can make parents feel extremely worried yet it can be both essential and beneficial for a child's well-being. Parents that we interviewed during our research for this book spoke positively about tube feeding once they had given it a try. Many parents shared how they noticed bene-fits from tube feeding in their child's overall well-being and energy levels once they were receiving the correct nutrients.

Tube feeding can be used to supplement oral food intake. If your child can safely eat and drink they may be encouraged to continue taking food orally whilst also receiving a feed via a tube. For many children being tube fed is a temporary measure, although it can be difficult to assess how long a tube feed may be needed for.

There are a number of different types of tube feeds and the one that is used will depend on your child's needs. These include:

✓ NG or naso-gastric – this runs from the nose to the stomach and is often used for short term tube feeding
✓ G or gastric – this tube is placed in the stomach through surgery
✓ NJ or naso-jejunal – this tube runs from the nose to the intestines and may be used as a trial before other tubes are considered

There are a number of other types of tube that are more rarely used. If your child is going to be tube fed it is important that the options are discussed with you and that you consider the pros and cons of each type of option before making a decision. You will receive training on how to clean equipment and how to administer feeds. There also will be the opportunity to practise tube feeding your child under medical supervision before you are left to feed your child alone.

Sophie has had four children who were all born prematurely. Each of her children has at some point been tube fed. Here she describes her experience of tube feeding:

" *Ella was my first home tube fed baby; she was taken into hospital for a fundoplication due to severe reflux and oxygen dependency because of chronic lung disease and aspiration pneumonia. After the six hours surgery I went to the recovery unit to be reunited with her and I saw what I now know is a gastrostomy tube. The tube was used to reintroduce food into her stomach. Ella refused to breastfeed and refused food after the surgery; she became fully tube dependent. I felt very helpless and sad because Ella had been a great feeder prior to surgery.*

We worked through a gastrostomy tube booklet alongside nursing staff and learnt to feed, flush and change the tube and what to do if the tube blocked and what to do if we could not get another tube in. Ella carried on being dependent on her tube until she was eight years old. The tube was removed at eight years six months after it had been redundant for four months. Tube feeding was a negative experience for Ella herself but the surgery was life-saving so that in itself is hugely positive. "

Sophie's son Eddie is now two years old:

" *When I was told that Eddie my son was to be tube fed it was a relief that he would no longer have to struggle and fight every breath; he had been having real difficulties with eating orally. I was also sad that we had just got rid of one tube as Ella had just started eating orally again and here we were with another one going in. I was relieved for Eddie when I was told that he needed to be tube fed and the expression on his face once the tube feeding was introduced showed that he was relieved too.*

Eddie has been tube fed for eighteen months now; it is still ongoing though he is gaining weight. Tube feeding has been a hugely positive experience for Eddie as he was grossly underweight; he desperately needed help so it was a huge relief when he finally got help. It was a relief to see him no longer struggling to eat and to know that there would be no more battling to get the calories in him.

We have had lots of support from professionals around tube feeding: we had a nurse visit every week, regular weigh-ins, a dietician visit and more surgical appointments. It was difficult to start with trying to juggle tube feeding, oxygen dependency and a child with cerebral palsy, but once we got used to the equipment it soon became normality! Every time we went out I needed to make sure we had a spare feeding tube, two of each size syringes, a naso-gastric tube, tape, a feeding pump and extension sets once the tube was changed to a button.

What I would say to other parents is that tube feeding isn't as bad as it seems even though it can seem scary at first. It takes all the pressure off trying to get food in a child and can have a real positive impact on your child's well-being. **"**

Vitamins and supplements

Most children can get the right amount of vitamins and minerals simply by eating a varied and healthy diet. If your child has eating issues, however, you may be concerned about their vitamin and mineral levels. It is essential that our bodies receive the correct nutrients in order to remain healthy. It is possible to use supplements if you cannot achieve the correct levels through diet alone. The Department of Health recommends that children aged six months to five years should take a vitamin A, C and D supplement as a precaution because growing children may not get enough of these vitamins via their diet, particularly if they are fussy eaters. If your child is under five years old you should seek the advice of your health visitor before offering additional supplements. For older children you should speak to your GP who may be able to recommend supplements to try. There has been a great deal of research carried out into food supplements and additional needs. It is best to seek advice from medical experts before trying something with your child.

Dr Pippa Rundle confirms that, 'A healthy diet should contain all the calories and vitamins necessary for normal growth and development. If a child has a restricted diet because of allergies or other illness then professional advice should be given about supplements, and growth and general health should be monitored.'

See Chapter 1 for more about vitamins and a healthy diet.

General tips

Here are some general tips to help children who have additional needs in relation to their eating. These tips will not be appropriate for all children as needs and understanding varies so greatly. It is helpful to identify tips that you may be able to put into practice for your child:

✓ Keep calm, your child will pick up on your stress and it is important that mealtimes remain calm and positive in order for progress to be made

✓ Give your child warnings that mealtimes are approaching. Some children find using a visual timetable helpful and this will be discussed in Chapter 8. If your child is engaged in an activity that they enjoy and may not wish to end you could forewarn them that in two minutes the activity needs to end so that they can have some food

✓ Some children find objects of reference useful to remind them of the time of day. You could select one that indicates 'mealtimes' to your child; this could be a piece of cutlery, a plate or even a bib

✓ Be consistent around mealtimes. Eat in the same place each mealtime and make sure that your child knows where they will be sitting and what equipment will be used

✓ Take your time at mealtimes and let your child have time to smell and touch the food if necessary

✓ Allow your child time to make choices relating to food. If they are fed by you, ask them what they would like to taste next

✓ Learning to eat can be messy, so accept that if your child is able to feed themselves there will be some mess involved. Break the process down into small steps; initially, you may need to load the spoon for them and let them pull it towards their mouth independently. Once this is mastered you can begin to teach them how to load the spoon by putting your hand over theirs to guide it. Cover the floor if necessary so that it doesn't matter if food is dropped, and invest in wipe-clean aprons

✓ Praise your child throughout mealtimes; make feeding a positive experience so that it becomes enjoyable, not dreaded!

Jayne tells us,

❝ *I never force my son's eating issues, as this does not work. I feel that even though his likes are limited, he does have a balanced diet and is very fit and healthy. It is more important that he enjoys his food now and has a good appetite; as he gets older he will hopefully accept more foods. I think that if you can find at least one food in each food group which your child enjoys then that is a good start.* **❞**

In summary

It is impossible to cover every condition and its impact on feeding in this one chapter as there are so many different syndromes and diagnoses that a child may have. If you are unsure as to whether your child's condition may have associated eating issues you can check out the medical information on Contact a Family's website. This covers a wealth of different conditions and gives a breakdown around symptoms: www.cafamily.org.uk.

If feeding is an issue, share this with professionals; they may be able to offer you advice around activities that you can carry out at home to help to develop your child's feeding and eating skills. Other parents who have been through similar situations can be a tremendous source of help. Find out about local parent support groups by asking at your child's school or children's centre, or by contacting your local Family Information Service or your local library.

Chapter 7
Food Allergies and Sensitivities

Food allergies and sensitivity to food have become far more common over the last decade. Statistics suggest that around 8% of children aged three and under now have a food allergy. The National Institute for Health and Clinical Excellence (NICE) has reported that hospital admissions for food allergies among children have risen in the last twenty years by 500%.

In this chapter we will investigate what exactly food allergies are and what symptoms children may present with if they have an allergy. We will also look at how to manage allergies and encourage your child to develop independence around managing their allergy if appropriate. Food intolerances are often confused with food allergies so we will also explore the difference and, again, how to manage these effectively.

There are still a surprising number of additives used in food and these can have a direct impact on children's behaviour. This chapter will make you aware of the use of these and offer guidance around how to avoid them in your child's diet.

Children with special needs may find that they are particularly sensitive to certain foods. Research has shown, for example, that food allergies can worsen symptoms in children with autism. If you suspect that your child has an allergy or is sensitive to certain food types it is important that you seek medical advice.

What is a food allergy?

A food allergy occurs when the body's immune system mistakes a certain type of food for a poison. The body then produces antibodies to guard against what it perceives as a harmful danger. This process is known as sensitization. At this stage there may be no symptoms displayed. The next time the food is eaten, however, the antibodies are produced and symptoms may be experienced. Food allergies often cause mild reactions although sometimes they can prove fatal. Food intolerance is different from a food allergy and will be discussed later on in this chapter.

Various foods can cause children to have allergic reactions: these may include nuts, cows' milk, eggs, fish and shellfish amongst various others. Whilst food allergies are more common in children than adults and it is possible to grow out of them, it is also possible to develop a food allergy in adulthood.

Sometimes having an allergy to one type of food can lead to a reaction with other products. This is known as cross-reactivity. Shelly tells us about her daughter who has an allergy to eggs:

" *Sophie has been diagnosed with a food allergy to eggs and we need to avoid them as she can become quite ill if she is in contact with them. Even just touching them while baking can cause a reaction. We've noticed that she also has a mild reaction if she eats chicken.* **"**

Why do allergies occur?

It still is not fully understood why children are allergic to different foods. Some food allergies appear after birth at a young age while other allergies seem to occur later during childhood. A child who has eczema or asthma is more at risk of having a food allergy. If there are allergies in the family a child will be at a higher risk of developing them.

What are the symptoms?

Symptoms that children display when they have a food allergy can vary from mild to severe and even life-threatening. Below are some of the more common symptoms to look out for:

✓ Swelling around the lips, mouth, tongue or throat
✓ Itching around the mouth
✓ Difficulties breathing
✓ Rashes or hives on the skin

✓ Feelings of nausea or vomiting
✓ Diarrhoea
✓ Abdominal swelling
✓ Coughing
✓ A runny nose
✓ Itchy eyes

Some children have extremely severe allergic reactions to food substances and these can be triggered by a child just being near to somebody eating that food or touching something that the food has been in. Stella is mum to Jack, aged four, who has a diagnosis of autism and also a food allergy to peanuts. She tells us:

" Jack's allergy is severe and he can't even touch an empty box that has contained cereals, for example, that have nuts in them. It means that school have to be very aware and make sure that when they do box modeling all of the packages are suitable to use. They have been very supportive and sent a letter home explaining that a pupil does have a severe nut allergy and asking parents to check that they don't send in boxes that have contained nut products. People think when a child has a nut allergy it just means that they can't eat nuts but it is actually more complex than that. I have to check everything for nuts as often food products may contain traces of nuts. I also have to make sure that nobody is eating anything containing nuts around him. "

If you suspect that your child has a food allergy it is important to consult your GP for advice. If you are aware of which food may have caused the reaction, avoid giving this to your child until you have taken medical advice. To help GPs diagnose food allergies in children NICE released guidelines in February 2011, called: 'Food allergy in children and young people: Diagnosis and assessment of food allergy in children and young people in Primary Care settings'. If your child is experiencing the symptoms of an allergy, ask your GP for referral to an allergy consultant in a specialist allergy clinic.

Anaphylaxis

Some people experience a severe allergic reaction that is referred to as anaphylaxis or anaphylactic shock. This is rare but requires urgent medical treatment as it can be life-threatening. Symptoms of anaphylactic shock include dizziness and a drop in pulse rate and blood pressure. The airways and throat or lips may swell making breathing difficult. A child with anaphylactic shock may have red, blotchy skin caused by the dilation of blood vessels. If anaphylactic shock is suspected emergency medical treatment should be sought immediately.

Anaphylactic shock can be triggered not only by eating certain foods such as nuts, milk and fish but also by insect stings such as bees and wasps. Certain medications can also cause anaphylactic shock.

Diagnosis of food allergies

When visiting your GP you should be prepared to clearly describe your child's symptoms. You may wish to consider whether they have displayed these symptoms before and, if so, how long this has being going on. If possible, describe how long symptoms take to appear after eating the food.

If your child displays symptoms immediately after eating the food then tests can be carried out to determine what they are allergic to. These include skin prick tests, whereby the skin is pricked and food extracts are placed on the skin. The forearm or back are usually used and if any redness or swelling occur around the site it indicates that an allergy is present. Blood tests called Specific IgE blood tests may also be carried out. Both of these tests should only be carried out by a qualified allergy specialist as the most important part of a diagnosis of a food allergy is in the clinical history that is taken before any tests are done. Do not be tempted to use tests advertised on the internet or high street as most of these have little or no scientific evidence to support them.

It is more difficult to test for food allergies when the symptoms are delayed. You may be asked to follow an exclusion diet where the suspected foods are removed from your child's diet, and you may be referred to a dietician in order to receive assistance with this process.

The symptoms will improve if there is a food allergy present. The food will then be reintroduced, and if symptoms return when your child begins eating the food again a diagnosis of a food allergy may be made.

Food allergies need testing for throughout childhood as it is possible that your child will grow out of the allergy and it may be possible to reintroduce the food at a later date.

Debbie is mum to Oscar and tells us:

" *I breastfed Oscar and felt that the midwife pushed me to top up with formula, which I tried a couple of times. Both times Oscar would be sick about seven to eight hours later. At three weeks, we then tried him on a different brand of formula and he vomited for hours and hours. We ended up in hospital as he had already lost over 10% in weight and we were really worried. We stayed in overnight and they did all sorts of tests. Once he had stopped being sick and they could find nothing wrong with him we were sent home. The staff that we saw wouldn't even consider that it was a food allergy. We were fairly convinced he was reacting to the milk and so self-diagnosed a problem with milk. I took milk out of my diet; when I would try adding it back in Oscar would get sick again. It was a very, very thick, curdled sick, not typical for a newborn. He also got a very nasty rash on his face. Again we went back to hospital and they gave antibiotics which helped clear it up but he was left with really bad skin that took weeks to really clear. He also had eczema all over his body. At one point we even paid to go privately and see a skin specialist. She did not mention food allergies but gave us loads of creams to try. When we started to wean him we tried him with bread and eggs. Both times he had reactions; he started vomiting and his skin erupted in hives, so we removed it from his diet. We had already been referred to an allergist by our supportive GP. They did blood tests and at twelve months old did skin prick tests. These showed that he had allergies to dairy, eggs and wheat. Even after all these allergens had been removed from both our diets he still slept badly and so we investigated more and then removed fruits with high fructose content. Oscar finally improved and at around sixteen months slept through the night. He now has a range of foods that he can eat and so we stick to them. He is fairly limited and also fussy so it is hard work but we get by.*

We had to use our instincts and do our own research around food allergies. I would say to parents that if you suspect that your child has an allergy look into it more thoroughly before dismissing the idea. **"**

Lauren's daughter Rachel has asthma and eczema and she was also concerned about food allergies:

" *I did wonder if she was allergic to dairy foods so we tried a dairy-free diet for a couple of weeks. This didn't seem to make a lot of difference but recently I discovered that citrus fruits can trigger it so she doesn't drink orange juice now. Interestingly, after not drinking orange juice for a while and then trying some, her mouth came up in a bit of a rash.* **"**

Living with food allergies

If your child has been diagnosed with a food allergy then the best course of action is to avoid that food altogether. Food allergies can have a huge impact on the whole family and on your child. Shopping habits may need to change and more time might need to be spent reading the labels of foodstuffs.

You will need to make others aware of your child's food allergy and also make them aware of the symptoms that your child suffers from, just in case they are given some food that they are allergic to when you are not present. Should they have an allergic reaction, some children may need antihistamine medicine; if your child is in school they need to have some medicine somewhere accessible just in case.

Depending on what your child is allergic to you may need to seek advice via a dietician to ensure that your child does not miss out on vital nutrients. It is possible to maintain a good nutritious diet even when a child has a number of food allergies, and dieticians are best placed to offer support around this. If you haven't been referred to a dietician yet feel this could be useful, speak to your child's GP or paediatrician about a referral. A dietician can also help you to identify alternative foods and suggest recipes to try at home.

It may be helpful for other family members if you make a list of what foods your child can eat and what must be avoided. Sometimes even certain *brands* of food can trigger an allergy. Robbie has a 5-year-old with a nut allergy and says, 'I can give Martha certain brands of chocolate and she is fine, yet with other brands she immediately suffers a reaction. I now have a banned and an allowed list of chocolate that I share with others so that they are very clear about what she can and can't eat as it does get confusing.'

Preparation is also important and you will need to take time to consider what meals you can prepare that are appropriate not only for your child but also for the rest of the family. Sometimes this might mean batch cooking and freezing portions if necessary. Planning menus in advance should help to make shopping trips more manageable.

You will find that you also need to plan ahead around social occasions if your child has a food allergy. Other parents will need to be aware of what your child can and can't eat and it is always a good idea to keep an emergency snack box to hand just in case you do arrive at a birthday party and find that your child's dietary requirements have been overlooked.

Allergy UK is a national charity dedicated to supporting those with allergies and food intolerances. They provide a national helpline (01322 619898) for advice and information, open Monday to Friday, 9 a.m.–5 p.m. You can also visit their website (www.allergyuk.org) for access to 130 downloadable factsheets on a range of allergic conditions including children's food allergies, as well as useful information such as a sample allergy protocol for your child's school or childcare staff. You can also access support around the clock on Allergy UK's online forum (http://forum.allergyuk.org). Allergy UK also provides translation cards in thirty languages with a tailored allergy alert message for peace of mind when you travel abroad, which can be ordered through their helpline.

Treating food allergies

There is, unfortunately, no cure for food allergies. The best form of treatment is to avoid the food that causes the allergy. Depending on the allergy it may be possible to use substitute foodstuffs, for example, using soya milk rather than dairy products for those children allergic to cows' milk.

Your child may be prescribed medication such as antihistamines or inhalers to help with symptoms. In more severe cases adrenaline-injecting devices may be required when there is a serious allergic reaction.

Gail's son is eight years old now and has an EpiPen because of a severe peanut allergy. She tells us about their situation:

" *Craig was eating a peanut butter sandwich at about fifteen months old; he'd already tried peanut butter before and had been fine with no reaction at all. On this occasion, however, his face began to swell up; he had to stay in hospital overnight and it was discovered that he had a very severe allergy for his age. He went on to have other tests and a mild allergy to raw egg was also discovered. In addition to his allergies Craig also has quite severe eczema and a tendency to suffer with breathing problems if he gets a cold.*

We carry EpiPens, and so do school. We have not had an attack now for over six years so it can be managed quite easily as long as you're sensible. We check food packets and he eats a lot of fresh food anyway so that's safer. We also managed to go away on a week's all-inclusive holiday when he was nineteen months old which had been booked a year previously so before he was diagnosed with the allergy. I was a bit worried but our travel company just approached the hotel beforehand and they were really good and said the only thing they couldn't guarantee was the ice cream. "*

Gail recognizes that it can be worrying when your child is away from you but says, 'The only time I do worry is, of course, when he's not with me and I have to hand responsibility for what he eats to someone else, but he went away overnight with Beavers earlier this year and that was fine and he's been to friends' houses without any issues.'

Tom also has an EpiPen because of a severe allergy to peanuts. His mum Sarah tells us how they cope living outside of the UK:

" *Tom has a severe allergy to peanuts and eggs. We carry an EpiPen at all times and he also has one in school with the nurse and in his classroom. Tom had his first and only major reaction to a tiny amount of peanut butter on toast on his first birthday. He was then put on the waiting list for testing and had another reaction while eating scrambled egg, thankfully though it was just bad hives and a bad flare-up of eczema. He had a Rast test to confirm the allergy: he is on the high score for the peanuts and medium still to egg; he is nearly six and has just been retested for egg through a skin prick and it came up very positive. We manage OK on a daily basis, but living in the Middle East is hard as there aren't labelling laws and nuts are served everywhere. We do not eat out with Tom as there is far too much of a risk. The best tip I can give to other parents is never take risks; it is not worth it; it is not fair on the sufferer. We do not have any nuts in the house or eggs and nothing that even contain traces. We are so very careful, but thankfully he hasn't had another reaction to peanuts since the first one. Thankfully Tom has a great class at school who do not make him feel left out at all. Parties can be a nightmare but we just take his own food. He has asked why he can't have things and we explain why. He knows he could die from eating certain foods; he probably doesn't understand completely, but he is a lovely boy and never ever accepts anything unless he has checked it is safe. He wears two bands; one says 'Allergy alert: please use EpiPen in emergency' and the other says 'Alert: severe food allergy, no eggs or nuts'. These are a godsend and he doesn't mind wearing them, thankfully.* "

Nadine Lewis is Director of ICE Gems, a company that produces medical jewellery. She tells us:

❝ *Children with allergies are often required to wear some form of medical identification, be it a bracelet or pendant. Medical alert jewellery can be a life-saving signpost to those administering first aid, helping to explain what type of allergy/allergies the child has and what course of action to take. They can, for example, highlight whether the child carries an EpiPen or antihistamine tablets as they have important In Case of Emergency (ICE) information engraved on them. Our bracelets have been designed with children in mind; they are fun and funky so that children want to wear them and don't feel that they are being stigmatized for having an allergy or medical condition. All ICE Gems medical jewellery has the globally recognized star of life symbol on the front which the emergency services are trained to look for and are engraved with the child's emergency contact and medical information on the reverse.* ❞

Food allergies in school

Your child's school will need to be made fully aware of any food allergies. If your child has a severe allergy then it is important that the school draw up a medical care plan. This will outline exactly what your child's issues are and how the symptoms may present. Guidance will be set out in the care plan to identify how the allergy will be dealt with in school if it happens to occur. A medical professional such as a school nurse should be responsible for drawing up the care plan. If you feel that a care plan is necessary for your child, ask to speak to the head teacher or SENCO who will be able to offer you further information.

Schools can cater for children with food allergies so this need not be a barrier to your child having a school meal alongside their peers. However, schools need to be made aware if you do have a child with a severe allergy that, for example, may be triggered by others eating the food product around them. A risk assessment may need to be carried out by the school of activities to ensure that cross-contamination of surfaces, for example, does not occur, in order to protect your child.

Supporting your child to develop independence

It is important that your child enjoys food despite their food allergy and they will need you as a parent to help them gain confidence in managing their issue if appropriate. Children with more severe learning and cognitive difficulties may remain reliant on carers to manage their food choices throughout their life. However, if your child has the ability to learn about their food allergy it is important that you support them in becoming as independent as possible in terms of managing their own diet.

You may wish to consider teaching your child about checking labels for safe foods to eat. If your child struggles to read you could consider whether they would be able to match words. If you produced reference cards, for example, containing the words that they need to look out for on labels they may be able to match these. Initially, your child will need a lot of support in order to develop these skills.

If your child will be dining independently in the future you should teach them about asking what is in the dishes when in cafes and restaurants. If necessary, you could provide them with a laminated sheet which outlines what their food allergies are so that this can be passed on to the chef, who can advise about suitable dishes to try.

Food Intolerance

Food intolerance is not the same as having a food allergy. An intolerance describes an adverse reaction to a foodstuff each time the food is eaten and particularly when eaten in larger quantities. The immune system, however, isn't activated as it is with a food allergy. Food intolerances occur because the body is unable to deal with certain types of food because it fails to produce enough of a particular enzyme or chemical to cope with digestion.

Many children have an intolerance for cows' milk. This is actually because of the lactose that is present in the milk, which is a type of sugar. Many children have a shortage of the enzyme lactase and without this they are unable to break down the lactose. Other common intolerances include those to preservatives and additives in food. Sometimes the lack of an enzyme can lead the body to mimic allergy symptoms so it is common for food intolerances and food allergies to become confused.

Food intolerances can be genetic. Lactose intolerance usually begins after the age of two but again symptoms may not be displayed until a child is much older. Sometimes children can temporarily develop a lactose intolerance following a bout of gastroenteritis.

Symptoms of food intolerance

Food intolerance symptoms can include the following:

- ✓ Nausea
- ✓ Bloating
- ✓ Diarrhoea
- ✓ Abdominal pain

Symptoms may begin quickly after eating or drinking the food in question, or even days afterwards. The intensity of symptoms will vary but food intolerances are usually harmless yet unpleasant.

Diagnosis and treatment

The easiest way to diagnose food intolerance is to cut the suspected food out of your child's diet and see if symptoms improve. There is, however, a specific test for lactose intolerance and your GP can carry this out if you feel this may be an issue.

Cutting the food out of your child's diet is the best way to manage a food intolerance. Alternatives can be used for those children who have lactose intolerance, such as giving soya or hypoallergenic milk rather than cows' milk. If food is cut out you should always make sure that suitable alternatives are used and again consult a dietician for advice if appropriate.

Food additives

Research shows that children's behaviour can be affected by food additives and children with ADHD and autism may be more likely to display hyperactive behaviour as a result of their diet. Additives have no nutritional value and are added simply to make food last longer, or look and taste better. Research has proven that, when artificial colours are taken out of food, children's behaviour improves.

Sometimes it is difficult to spot additives in food as they may not be listed in the ingredients. Also, print can be small and the list may use their name or E number. You may see some additives listed simply as 'flavourings' on food labels. Some food may also be sold without packaging, such as baked products and takeaway meals. Additives can even be found in children's medicine.

The majority of processed foods in the UK contain additives. While some are used to preserve the food for longer, others are used to make products more quickly, or even to bulk out food. Around 90% of food additives are used purely for cosmetic purposes.

Netmums has produced a downloadable shopping list to print off that outlines the additives to avoid. This is a really useful resource to have with you if you are trying to eliminate additives from your child's diet; you can find it on their website at www.netmums.com and by searching for 'food additives' online.

Food sensitivity

Some parents that we have spoken to during our research have described their children as being sensitive to certain types of food. A sensitivity is not the same as an allergy or intolerance. Children with a sensitivity may find that their behaviour is affected after eating certain foods.

David is father to James who is now twelve years old and has learning difficulties. He tells us:

" *When James was younger he was constantly drinking and on the go. He was almost addicted to fresh orange juice. I actually encouraged this as I thought that fresh fruit juice was a healthy option and that it would do him good. His behaviour was very hyperactive and he'd run around for hours; he never seemed to get tired. His sleep pattern was extremely poor and his concentration levels were low. I never actually considered that it could be the orange juice that was leading to this behaviour. I have always been keen to provide my children with a good, balanced* *diet so it didn't occur to me that he may be food sensitive. Once we cut out the orange juice his behaviour improved and he became much calmer.* 🥇

Sarah has a 15-year-old daughter with severe learning difficulties. It was her school that first suggested that she may have a food sensitivity. Sarah tells us:

🥇 *Donna has always had challenging behaviour but her teacher noticed that on certain days in the afternoon she was far worse. She would often come back to the classroom after dinner time in an agitated state and lash out at children and staff. After careful observation her teacher decided to keep a log of what she was eating at lunchtime. It quickly became apparent that on the days that she chose strawberry mousse her behaviour deteriorated and there appeared to be a direct link.* 🥇

In summary

If you suspect that your child has an allergy, sensitivity or intolerance to food it is important to seek medical help. You should mention your concerns to your GP or paediatrician at the first opportunity. It is also important that you do not make drastic changes to your child's diet without taking advice from professionals: your child still needs to have access to appropriate levels of nutrition in order to promote their well-being. Allergies are on the increase for all children including those with special needs.

Keeping a food diary can be helpful in monitoring allergies, intolerances and sensitivities. The next chapter will look at food diaries along with offering ideas to help to make food fun once more.

Chapter 8
First Steps to Making Food Fun Again

When your child has an eating issue the pleasure can quickly be taken away from mealtimes. Food plays such an important role in our lives that it is important that children are encouraged to explore the pleasure of food. In this chapter we will look at how to keep food diaries and the important information that they can provide you with. We will also explore games and activities that encourage children to develop a healthier relationship with food. We will speak to a range of experts in this field and get their top tips for making mealtimes fun once more.

Nutritionist Charlotte Stirling-Reed tells us:

" *For many children with special needs, food can be a little daunting and mealtimes especially can be a potentially scary time. Unfamiliar foods create anxiety, meaning that often children with special needs have very restrictive diets. Introducing games and activities that are centred on food as early as possible can really help to familiarize children with foods and make them feel much more comfortable trying new varieties.* "

Food diaries

Food diaries are a really important way of keeping track of what your child is eating. Children's appetites vary from day to day and from week to week. Charlotte Stirling-Reed, owner of SR Nutrition and a registered public health nutritionist advises that:

" *It is important not to worry too much about how much or how little your child is eating in a single day, and instead to try and look at what has been eaten throughout a whole week: a diary is the best way to monitor your child's food intake.*

Food diaries not only help to keep an important record of

your child's weekly food intake but can also be used as a fun food activity to help with your child's learning process. 🔎

If possible, Charlotte advocates involving your child in completing their own food diary. She says:

🔎 *Although for parents, keeping track of what their little one eats is good practice, it is also a great idea to get children involved by filling out a food diary for themselves. This can help children to familiarize themselves with mealtime routines, learn about different foods and will, additionally, help them to think about all the different foods they have eaten and enjoyed throughout the day. Routine is a really important principle in encouraging children with special needs to eat a healthy diet and keeping a food diary can go a long way to helping your children accept this routine.* 🔎

Charlotte offers the following tips to help you to complete a food diary:

✓ When filling in a food diary, it is useful to try to write as much detail as possible about the foods that have been eaten during that day
✓ Remember to record any snacks or drinks that are eaten in between meals, ensuring that the food diary really is a true reflection of what has been eaten
✓ If your child attends school or nursery during the day, try to get a daily report on the foods that were offered, how the mealtime went and how much was eaten, so that you can add it to the food diary and ensure you are filling it in appropriately
✓ When filling out the food diary encourage your child to share thoughts and feelings, if possible, about the foods that they have eaten. This is especially important if they didn't like the food or felt anxious eating it for any particular reason
✓ Keep an account of any activity your child takes part in during the day, so you can also see if they are getting enough regular exercise. Again, be sure to ask carers or school staff if you are

not sure how much activity they participate in when away from the home

✓ Where possible, encourage your child to fill out their own food diary, using lots of pictures to keep them interested in the task and to familiarize them with different types of food. You can use pictures of the food to stick onto the food diary as a method of recording what your child has eaten and then refer back to this when the food is on the menu again at a later date

In Chapter 12 you will find examples of food diaries that you can adapt for your child.

Kate Barlow is a parent consultant at www.parentconsultancy.com. She explains how to use the data that you gather from your food diaries:

" *Parents sometimes find that their children are eating a lot more than they originally thought once they have kept a food diary. If you see that your child is snacking more than necessary, reduce the number of snacks that they have between meals. Children can get into the habit of grazing, which means that they don't have the chance to build an appetite between meals. Alternatively, it might be that you need to change the times of meals; a child who is tired or has a meal too close to snack time will not eat as well. Use the diary too to look at the type of foods that your child is eating as a snack. Snacks should be an energy boost between meals, but crisps, biscuits, cakes and sweets can fill up children and provide little nutrients. Offer fruit, breadsticks, cheese or crudités in order to give your child an energy boost without spoiling their appetite.* **"**

A balanced diet

We know how important a balanced diet is for well-being but sometimes getting children to eat a balanced diet can be a challenge. Kate Barlow advises that it can be helpful to encourage children to be involved in food preparation: 'Children will often say that they do not like foods that are unfamiliar to them; try to encourage them in getting involved in the preparation of their food where possible. They may be able to assist you with the cleaning and chopping of vegetables, for example, and encourage them to taste the vegetables before they appear on their plate.'

Kate also suggests that food can be cooked in different ways as a means of introducing a more varied diet. She says:

" *Offer meals cooked, prepared and presented in a variety of different ways. Just because your child disliked their chicken grilled doesn't mean that they will dislike chicken roasted with gravy, which is in fact easier to chew. Some children prefer raw vegetables to cooked vegetables and vice versa. A child should be offered a type of food at least ten times before you can say they dislike it. Never replace a missed meal with a snack or a different meal as this will reduce the variety of food eaten by your child. They will always want their favourites.* "

Introducing new foods can take time. Kate advises, 'Introduce new foods gradually and in small portions; remember that the more familiar your child is with the food, the more likely they are to eat it. Don't be disheartened if your child takes time to get used to eating new foods; it is important that you are consistent.'

There are many ways that you can encourage your child to eat more fruit and vegetables and make this fun. Here are some simple suggestions to try:

✓ Make milkshakes containing fresh fruit
✓ Use dips and raw vegetables to encourage them to experiment with different flavours
✓ Make pizzas with smiley vegetable faces
✓ Add dried fruit to cereals at breakfast time
✓ Make smoothies in different flavours and give them fun names
✓ Pancakes are fun to make and fruit can be added as a topping
✓ Use different shaped cutters to make the food appear to be more interesting
✓ Grow your own fruit or vegetables and encourage your child to help you while they grow

Claudia has a daughter who is currently under assessment for special educational needs and has always been a selective eater. She says:

" *Imogen started to get fussy with her food when she was around three years old. I used to get really upset and worried about her not eating enough and not getting the right vitamins. She has always refused to eat any fruit and vegetables, which was a real worry for me. We saw a dietician who gave me tips on how to make food more fun. I have to be honest, at first I was really reluctant to implement the ideas as I felt that she should just eat the food put in front of her. I did, however, concede and actually find myself now really enjoying preparing her meals. I make fruit kebabs, for example, and she loves these. If, however, I gave her the fruit just chopped up onto a plate she would not eat it. I also make her fruit cocktails to drink; they have fresh fruit juice in them and I put a cherry and a cocktail umbrella on the side. She sees these as a treat and it helps me to make sure that her fruit intake remains at an appropriate level.* "

Melissa Hood, director of the Parent Practice, offers the following advice:

✓ Show your child pictures of new foods – a study carried out by Dr Carmel Houston-Price, of the School of Psychology and Clinical Language Science at the University of Reading, which was reported in December 2009, found that exposure to pictures of fruit and vegetables could be key to encouraging youngsters to sample new tastes. In the study children were shown books containing images of fruit not familiar to them, such as lychees. The toddlers then took part in 'a willingness to taste test' where, overall, the children were more interested in tasting unfamiliar foods if they had previously seen pictures of them in books

✓ Let them choose – another way of encouraging healthy eating is by having a fruit bowl somewhere accessible. If you vary the fruit that you buy, your child will become used to seeing different types of fruit and have a variety to choose from. Let your child choose a new fruit or vegetable at the supermarket and chat about where it comes from. Some parents have reported that it made all the difference when their child chose which piece of broccoli they were going to buy. Again, the more familiar they become, the more likely they are to eventually eat it!

✓ Make it look familiar – try serving new foods in a similar way to old favourites. So, for example, if one of your child's favourite meals is chicken in a creamy sauce try serving fish in the same creamy sauce. Or if they enjoy eating chips, try sweet potato chips instead. The more familiar they are, the more likely they are to try it

✓ Provide variety – try cooking or presenting things in different ways. A child who doesn't like boiled or steamed vegetables may like them stir-fried or roasted or, even better, raw. Conversely, a child who doesn't touch a raw apple may love a baked one. Some children don't like diced or sliced carrots but will lap them up if they're grated. And yet others will eschew the florets of broccoli in favour of the stalks. Lots of kids don't like sauce smothering their food but may be willing to dip into a sauce bowl

✓ Disguise food – if your child likes sauces, of course, you can hide a lot of vegetables in them. Every parent knows of the wonders of bolognese sauce or cottage pie for hiding veggies in! See Chapter 4 for an important note of caution about hiding food

Texture of foods

Some children will have issues around eating foods of different textures. For some children this is a sensory integration issue, as outlined in Chapter 4. Other children may have sensory issues as a result of an autism spectrum disorder. Some children can have issues around the texture of foods because of physical conditions such as dental problems or swallowing difficulties. Some children, however, may simply have a temporary issue around foods of a certain texture.

Children can be described as having issues around textures of food if they will only eat food of a certain consistency, for example, they will only eat foods that are smooth such as yoghurt, custard and cream cheese. Some children will only eat hard foods such as carrots, apples and celery. If you are worried about your child's issues around the texture of food you should always seek medical advice.

If your child prefers smooth foods you can use a blender to introduce them to different tastes and flavours at a consistency that they
will tolerate. Allowing your child the opportunity to touch their food
can also be helpful when introducing different food textures.

Smell and food

Some children are extremely sensitive to the smell of food. If your
child dislikes the smell of a certain food it is highly unlikely that they
are going to eat it. You can offer your child the chance to touch and
smell the food prior to serving it, but you should not force a child to
eat something that they do not find appetizing.

Food choices

Hazel is an experienced special needs teacher who has worked with
a range of children aged between two and nineteen years with additional needs and feeding issues. Hazel tells us that it is important to
give children food choices:

*" Children should not be forced to eat any food, this will only
lead to them becoming anxious and stressed. It is a good idea
to offer children a choice of two different foods; this helps them
to feel more in control. So, for example, if you want to serve
some vegetables ask your child 'do you want peas or broccoli?'
You can show them the food too to support their understanding.
The 'when – then' rule is also useful to use at mealtimes. It is
much more positive to say to a child, 'When you have finished
your meal, then you can go out to play' than saying, 'You aren't
going out to play until you've eaten your meal'. "*

Separate foods

Some children insist on having their food presented in a certain way.
Many children cannot tolerate food touching another type of food on
their plate: some adults also have certain rules that must be followed

when serving their food. If your child has issues around food touching on their plate you may wish to consider serving portions up on separate dishes.

Finger foods

Finger foods can help children develop and maintain their independence skills around eating, particularly if they have motor control issues. If your child needs to be fed you may consider whether using finger foods at some meals is a possibility to help them to be less dependent on others and to increase their self-esteem. This also allows your child to eat at a speed that they feel comfortable with rather than being fed, while allowing them to make their own choices about what they would like to eat next.

There are many different types of finger foods that you can offer your child. These may include the following:

✓ Sandwiches
✓ Crackers
✓ Crumpets
✓ Cereal bars
✓ Chicken or fish dippers
✓ Pizza slices
✓ Hotdogs or hamburgers
✓ Fresh or dried fruit
✓ Vegetables such as carrot sticks and cauliflower heads
✓ French fries or potato wedges

Portion size

Kate Barlow advises parents to consider portion sizes carefully. She says, 'Offer your child a small portion to begin with and shower them with praise when they have finished. You can increase the portion size and they will get into the habit of finishing meals this way. Respect your child's appetite and when they say they have had enough to eat don't try to get them to eat more.' Kate believes firmly in offering positive reinforcement to children. She says, 'Reward charts can be helpful to encourage eating if your child responds well to stickers. Often, however, verbal praise is enough.'

Incentives and rewards

There are many ways that you can reward your child around their eating but you should always make sure that what you are offering is a reward and not bribery or a punishment. You know your child better than anybody else so it is important to take some time to consider what kind of reward or incentive may be motivating to them. Children will only respond positively to a reward if they want the reward. Sue is mum to Alex who is eleven years old. She tells us how a well-meaning member of staff at her daughter's school tried to reward her eating but got it badly wrong.

" *Alex has always been a good eater and very mature for her age. I was surprised when school got in touch to say that she was leaving her meals at lunchtime. I had a word with Alex and eventually she told me that if she ate all her lunch the midday supervisor, as a reward, let her dine on what they called the Top Table. This meant eating alongside the head teacher and away from her friends. Alex was really quite distressed about this and didn't view it as a reward at all. She therefore started to leave her lunch so that she wouldn't be one of the chosen children. Once I'd realized this I was able to let the school know and they adapted the reward policy immediately.* **"**

Rewards should be:

- ✓ Positive
- ✓ Motivating
- ✓ Given with consistency
- ✓ To keep, never taken away
- ✓ Achievable: you need to explain to your child what you expect from them
- ✓ Simple, so that your child understands them
- ✓ Given immediately

Rewards don't have to be material items although sometimes it is nice to use a sticker or a small toy as a treat. Rewards should not be food items; it is important to encourage your child to have a healthy relationship with food, not see it as a way of rewarding or denying themselves. One of the best rewards that you can give your child is your attention. Simply telling your child that they have behaved well at mealtimes and that you are proud of them is often enough. You need to be explicit in what you are rewarding so starting your sentence with 'I like the way you . . .' can be useful. Your child needs to know what aspect of their behaviour you are pleased with so that they can repeat it.

You cannot force your child to eat, and using punishments if your child doesn't eat can be damaging. If your child's eating issue is behaviour-based then punishing them will not support them to change their behaviour. Children respond more positively to rewards than they do to sanctions so it is important to keep positive about eating issues even if, on the inside, you are feeling negative. If your child picks up on your negativity this will continue the negative cycle. Nicole Freeman runs cookery classes for children. Here she tells us about the importance of rewards:

" Persuade kids to try something new and reward them for doing so, even if they don't like it! The key thing is that they have tried it. At The Kids' Kitchen, we give children a certificate for all the new foods they have tried, and it's amazing how motivating this can be and how proud the kids are to show parents what they have tried. You can easily make your own reward chart at home or try a passport theme – give them a different fruit or veg 'stamp' when they've tried something new and let them build up their own fruit and veg passport. "

Games

Mealtimes need to be fun times and you may wish to consider whether it is appropriate to play games during your meal. A game can be something such as inventing a funny name for the dish that you are eating, or perhaps a game of 'I spy'.

Mealtimes should be an occasion where families catch up with each other so you could take time to listen to what each member of the family has been doing during the day. Or you could bring more structure to conversation by offering a sentence such as 'the funniest thing I've ever seen was . . .' and getting each member to complete the sentence.

Grow your own food

Growing your own food can be extremely rewarding and may motivate your child to eat. You don't even have to have a garden to be able to grow your own food. Cress is a great choice as a starting point as it grows very quickly and simply needs to be placed on a windowsill. You can grow cress in old boiled egg shells: wash them out and fill them with damp cotton wool and seeds, then draw a picture of a face on the front to create a 'cress head'. Or line some plastic trays with damp kitchen roll and then encourage your child to sow the cress seeds into shapes and watch them grow.

Visit your local garden centre and you will see a wide range of seeds available to purchase. You will also be able to buy child-size gardening tools to help to motivate your youngster; a trowel and a watering can are the two essential items. Initially, you should look at buying seeds that germinate quickly so that they see some reward for their efforts. Growing your own food is a great hobby for families to share, and home-grown food tastes wonderful, is fresher than anything that you can buy and is also cheaper.

Nicole Freeman, owner of Kids' Kitchen, says:

" *Kids are fascinated by watching something they've planted grow, and you can then use their produce in a recipe. And similarly, if there's a local pick-your-own farm near you that's a great way of getting kids involved and making cooking fun. Kids love eating something that they've picked and then cooked themselves. My kids now love beetroot as they have so much fun pulling it out of the ground at the farm, and making jam from strawberries and raspberries we've picked is one of our favourite summer activities.* **"**

Parental attitudes

Your attitude about food and mealtimes is incredibly important. Your child will view you as a role model so it is key that you are positive about mealtimes. You may need to listen carefully to yourself to see whether you are speaking in a positive manner about food and passing on a healthy message to your child. All too often we as adults speak negatively about food. Phrases like 'I've been good today so I can have a pudding' can lead children to have an unhealthy relationship with food, believing that it is there to be used as a reward. Melissa Hood, director of the Parent Practice, has the following tips to help to support you while managing your child's eating issues:

✓ Don't obsess. This is especially hard for mothers as nurturing our children is instinctive and fulfils primal needs
✓ Parents transmit their own attitudes toward food to their children so be careful what you say in front of them. 'Loose talk' creates attitudes to food for life. Don't talk about being fat or reproach yourself for what you eat or hide what you eat from someone else. For example, avoid saying things like, 'Don't tell Daddy I had this chocolate.' Don't talk about calories or whether food is fattening so much as whether it is healthy
✓ When we try too hard to encourage children to eat a particular amount of a particular food, in a particular way, we set the stage for a struggle for power and control. Our stress levels rise, and so do their stress levels, and mealtimes become a flashpoint of negative attention and negative behaviour
✓ Don't try to make children feel guilty to get them to eat. It doesn't work and will make them resentful
✓ Tell your child about why food is good for them: how protein builds muscle, calcium is good for bones, fish gives you brain power, vegetables provide vitamins, etc. But do this away from mealtimes or when they are eating the food under discussion, not when they've just refused it, or you will be giving too much negative attention to their eating
✓ Descriptively praise them for making healthy choices and for other good behaviour around mealtimes

Wendy Tomlinson is a life skills and law of attraction coach with a specialist interest in supporting parents and children. Wendy shares with us the importance of keeping calm:

** *When your child is tense about something and you become tense it can have a volcano effect where one or other of you is likely to explode. The law of attraction works on the basis that whatever we give our attention to the most we will attract. So if your child doesn't eat the amount of food that you would like and you focus your attention on this, you will actually attract more of this behaviour. This is the time when you need to keep calm.* **

Wendy offers the following tips for staying calm:

✓ Create a positive reminder book, a notebook that you decorate with a lovely photograph of your child, and write down in it all the great things about your child. Leave some pages blank so that you can add more. On a clean page write down how you want your child to behave, for example, 'My child sits at the table calmly at mealtimes' or 'My child eats a healthy balanced diet.' These are positive affirmations that will support the behaviour and outcome you desire. Read through your reminder book and focus on the behaviour that you want to see at mealtimes

✓ Plan to keep calm before mealtimes. Take a minute to relax by taking a few deep breaths and saying 'I am calm and relaxed'. Repeat this a few times; it is a great affirmation to use if you feel anxious during a mealtime too

✓ Keep positive: your positive vibes will be felt by your child and will help them to feel positive too

✓ Our self-talk can be very destructive at times. You may find yourself thinking things like 'I dread mealtimes' or 'I know he'll mess with his food again.' Whenever you recognize that you are having a negative thought, change it to a more positive thought, for example, 'He's not sitting still' can be changed to 'It's fantastic that he's sitting at the table'

✓ Lead by example; behave in a way that you want your child to follow. A parent who is constantly complaining during mealtimes is not a good role model. Relax, tell your child what you want in an upbeat positive voice and remain calm. Focus on what you want to happen and be grateful when it does, even if it's just for a short time. Keep focusing on these achievements and they become more and more frequent

You can read more about Wendy's work by logging on her site at www.wendytomlinsoncoaching.com/parenting.

In summary

In this chapter we have started to explore ways of making mealtimes fun and methods of motivating your child to eat and develop a healthier relationship with food. All of the suggestions are simple to try at home and aim to make food fun for all the family. In the next chapter we will explore more tips to try to encourage positive mealtimes.

Chapter 9
The Next Steps

We have started to look at positive steps that you can take to make food fun again. In this chapter we are going to explore more practical solutions to help to make mealtimes more enjoyable for the whole family both within the home and when dining out.

Melissa Hood, director of the Parent Practice, tells us:

" *Mealtimes can be an opportunity for families to come together to share experiences and to seek support from each other. They should be times for laughter and making happy memories and provide a great forum for teaching children things about life. This is what parents generally want from mealtimes but it is all too easy for them to turn into occasions of nagging and criticizing and sometimes shouting.* **"**

It is important that mealtimes do remain a positive experience for the whole family. In order to achieve this it may be necessary to plan mealtimes. You may need to consider how to structure meals and adopt new strategies. This chapter will offer you some ideas to support more positive dining.

The eating environment

Consider whether the environment that your child is eating in is the most suitable one. Ideally your child should eat at a table without the distraction of television. Mealtimes should be fun and positive with a good atmosphere. If your child hasn't been used to eating at a table it may take some time for them to accept that this is now where food will be served. They may resist the change initially but it is important that you keep firm boundaries in place and return them to the table if they walk away.

Children learn a great deal of their eating behaviours from adults.

It is important that you sit and eat with your child so that they can see how they should behave at the table. It is also a wonderful time to catch up as a family. A parent or carer is the most important role model in a child's life and a great source of learning. If you have a healthy attitude towards food and mealtimes your child is more likely to have one too.

Children with special needs thrive on routine: it can help them to make sense of the world. Get into the routine of sitting at the table with each family member having their own place. You may choose to give your child a plate with a favourite TV character on it in order to increase their appreciation of mealtimes.

Andrea has two boys with additional needs. She says:

❝ I do insist on the boys eating at the table: before they used to walk around the house eating which didn't work as they were constantly grazing, not to mention the mess it created! I thought this was the easier option as they refused to sit but I just persisted with it. Now they see this as part of their much-needed routine and are happy to sit at the table and eat. It was difficult getting them to this stage but worth it. They now both eat healthier meals and it is easier for me to keep track of what they have eaten. ❞

Alongside training your child to stay at the table, there can still be scope for fun mealtimes. Melissa Hood suggests eating in different environments. She says, 'Try a picnic in the garden, or the park. Don't wait for summer; you can wrap up warm, take a torch and some hot food such as baked potatoes wrapped in foil. If it's really dark and wet and miserable make a den in another room or under the table and have the picnic there.'

Melissa also suggests involving your child in preparing the meal-time environment.

❝ The children could also be involved in decorating the table maybe to a theme or with flowers. You probably won't do this every day but you could nominate one evening a week. You might play soft music during the mealtime. Music is very good

at creating mood so gentle music will calm things down rather than lively fast-paced music, which might be good for when it is time to clear away. 〞

Time at the table

The length of time for which a child will sit at the table will be dependent on the individual and their needs. If your child is a slow eater they may need to stay at the table for longer. The length of time that they are able to stay at the table will also depend on other factors such as how tired they are. For children who are struggling to sit at the table you may use a timer and ask them to stay until the timer sounds. It is important that they are rewarded for sitting at the table if they find this challenging. You can then gradually extend the amount of time by thirty seconds until your child learns to sit for a suitable period. It is important that you are realistic about the length of time a child will sit to eat a meal.

Visual timetables

Some children respond well to using a visual timetable to support their understanding around mealtimes. A visual timetable is a way of showing your child what is going to happen and in what order. Visual timetables can be made using photographs, symbols, pictures or words depending on your child's understanding. Using sticky-back Velcro on laminated card means that the pictures can be removed once each task has been completed. Children generally enjoy this activity: you can make a 'finished' box for them to post each picture into once it is complete.

Visual timetables can be used in a number of different ways at mealtimes. If your child uses a visual timetable in school it is worth finding out what kind of materials are used so that you can duplicate this at home. The number of pictures used will depend on your child's understanding; you should start off with just a couple and then add to these as your child masters using the timetable.

An example of a mealtime visual timetable could include pictures of:

✓ Washing hands
✓ Sitting at the table
✓ Eating the main course
✓ Having a drink
✓ Eating a pudding
✓ Leaving the table

Visual representation can also be used in order to encourage children to make choices at mealtimes. You may wish to set up a choosing book that contains symbols representing favourite foods. For example, a breakfast page could include pictures of toast, cereals, fruit, porridge and so on. Your child can then select the picture that they want in order to communicate their preferences.

Making mealtimes fun

Mealtimes can be made fun times very easily. It is important that children don't become distracted from their eating but it is possible to get a balance. Melissa Hood shares with us ideas that she has seen working well for families:

❝ *It is important to get the kids involved with ideas for making mealtimes special. One family I know have a theme for Friday Family Fun nights and they dress up according to the theme. Recently they chose an Olympic theme and each came dressed in sports kit. Another time they all dressed in their pyjamas! Some families play a game called 'Guess Who' which goes something like this: 'Guess who came to the table immediately when they were called?' Whoever did puts up their hand. 'Guess who is bravely trying their broccoli?' 'Guess who is eating in small mouthfuls?' 'Guess who is using his spoon and fork?' If you can't detect any good behaviour in front of you think of something that happened earlier in the day. 'Guess who made their bed this morning/fed the dog/didn't complain when she had her hair brushed?' Children are programmed to get our attention and we generally give them far too much attention for the wrong kind of behaviour, thus encouraging them to do more of what we don't want.* 🥟

Thinking creatively about how to make mealtimes fun is important. You know your child's interests and what will be motivating for them. Melissa suggests:

“ *You could play games which don't involve any equipment at the table provided they don't distract the children too much from eating: word games, alphabet games of every description or continuous stories or I spy. These games can work but you may need a rule that they have to finish their mouthfuls before speaking if it is a value for you that they don't speak with their mouths full. Try a story tea when you read a chapter from a favourite book while they eat.*

One family encouraged their daughter to use her napkin by asking her to pretend that she was a princess, kissing her napkin and blowing kisses to her adoring public, which she loved to do! There is no limit to parents' creativity. Many of us have made dwarf trees out of broccoli for our giant children to gobble up or made faces out of mashed potato and peas. You can even buy plates with faces printed onto them. I know my lifelong fondness of Brussels sprouts comes from the fact that I was told they were fairy cabbages ....I was hooked. **”**

Rob has a son with global developmental delay and he agrees that mealtimes should be fun:

“ *I was brought up where mealtimes were a chore and a dull occasion. I remember dreading them as a child. When we had Archie I realized I was doing the same sort of thing with him and insisting on him sitting at the table for periods of time that weren't realistic. I was nagging him to eat everything on his plate and generally making mealtimes unpleasant for us all. I changed my approach and realize now that mealtimes don't have to be that way. It is OK to play games at the table. Archie loves mealtimes now and I must admit my partner and I look* *forward to them much more. I think sometimes it is about trying a different approach.* **"**

Modelling eating

Adults can provide a good role model for children around developing good eating habits. Melissa Hood says:

" *We recommend that parents eat with their children whenever they can so that they can model good eating and train their children in the mealtime habits they want to see. Mealtimes are also a good way of spending positive time with children. If children are very young they may need to eat earlier than parents. If this is the case then try to have a lunchtime or a breakfast meal together over the weekend. When the kids eat earlier on weekdays an adult should sit with them to talk of pleasant things and notice their good behaviours. The dinner table is not the place to introduce difficult topics or talk about problems. You don't want food to be associated with negativity.*

When trying to get children into good habits it's a good idea to train them in small steps. Often this means starting with something easy. It might be advisable to start your new training regime with a meal that you know they all like while you address other rules of the table. Ask the children what the rules are – you may be surprised to learn that they actually already know what's expected of them. Give lots of descriptive praise for following the rules. **"**

Making changes to mealtimes

It may be that you need to review your family mealtimes in order to identify positive ways that you can make changes. Melissa offers the following advice about implementing change:

" *Create some space between the old regime and the new by having meals somewhere else for a couple of days. When you start up again change some of the things associated with the* *old ways, such as where the kids sit or their place mats or crockery. This will subconsciously signify change.*

Tell them that you are going to try your best not to nag or criticize and tell them what behaviour you expect of them. Obviously this conversation is age and cognitive ability dependant but don't assume that younger children or youngsters with learning difficulties can't take part. Write some rules down or put them into picture form. These should be positively framed and specific such as 'Sit with my bottom on the chair; leave toys behind; taste food even if I think I won't like it; eat with a fork and spoon/knife; keep my plate in front of me; say please and thank you, or ask to get down from the table'. Maybe take photos of the kids doing what they should and put the photos on a chart. When anybody does what's required (including you), acknowledge it. 'Joshua is trying something new.' 'Gemma has taken her plate over to the dishwasher.' 'Samantha, that was a lovely story you told us all about Grace, and you waited until your mouth was empty before you talked.' Some families keep a jar handy into which they put tokens such as pasta pieces whenever anyone does anything good. It is particularly successful because it is visual and it is a lot less effort than a praise or reward chart. When the jar is full maybe everyone could play a game together or go on an outing. "

Children with additional needs will have to overlearn rules. It may take longer for them to realize what they are supposed to be doing and how to behave. Keep positive and remember to reward the behaviours that you *do* want to see. Using the phrase 'I like the way ...' is helpful, so, for example, tell them 'I like the way you are sitting calmly at the table' or 'I like the way that you are eating with your mouth closed.' This will help your child to recognize exactly what behaviours they need to replicate in order to please you.

Dining out

Eating out with children can be extremely stressful, so much so that some families avoid it completely. If you would like to eat out with your child, Melissa tells us:

" *It may be obvious but choose a child-friendly restaurant. That doesn't necessarily mean the food on the menu, but more how they view children. The presence of a children's menu is a good indicator as is the décor. White tablecloths and wine glasses on the table may be a predictor of a stressful meal. Having chosen the restaurant, pack a bag. You know there will be a wait for the meal so take some things to keep your children occupied. Before you go ask the children how they will need to behave. Get a lot of detail from them about all elements of the visit, especially those that could go wrong: the waiting period, if they need to go to the toilet, choosing from the menu, what to do if they don't have anything you like, staying at the table, speaking to the waiter, making conversation and so on. If they say how they need to behave they are more likely to do it than if you just lecture them. Some families who have had problems in restaurants have used role play at home to practise how to behave in public eateries. This can be a useful exercise for children with limited understanding or who get anxious about new situations.* "

The social side of eating can also add an extra pressure to children with additional needs. Going out for a meal can be particularly difficult for them and many families that we have spoken to shared that they avoided eating out if at all possible. Here are some tips to help to make eating out less stressful:

✓ Try to choose a time that won't be too busy when dining out
✓ Book in advance and if possible identify the table that you feel would best suit your family's needs
✓ Examine the menu to see whether there is suitable food for your child. If not, explain to the staff about your child's feeding needs to see how they can be accommodated
✓ Make sure your child has things to do that interest them while waiting for their food

✓ Use visual prompts if necessary to explain to your child what is happening

✓ Have some snacks to hand in case there is a long wait and your child becomes impatient

✓ Keep calm; your child will pick up on your stress levels

Social Stories

A Social Story may be useful in supporting your child's understanding of dining out and mealtimes. A Social Story describes a situation and shares accurate information so as to enhance understanding of events. They can be particularly useful for children who have difficulty understanding social interaction and are frequently used with children who are on the autism spectrum. You can read more about Social Stories by visiting www.thegraycenter.org.

Sian uses Social Stories to support her daughter's understanding of mealtimes. She tells us, 'I find that Social Stories are really helpful, especially if we are going out for a meal. Simone enjoys listening to the stories and I have noticed that her behaviour has improved as a result of them. She seems to understand more about what is expected of her. I'd definitely recommend that other parents give them a try.'

In summary

This chapter has provided you with some practical tips to make mealtimes more manageable. Dining out can be stressful but with some careful preparation some of the stress can be alleviated. Be realistic about what your child can achieve at mealtimes. Setting targets can be helpful but they must be attainable. Make sure that your child receives plenty of praise for their positive mealtime behaviour.

Chapter 10
Cooking Together

Encouraging your child to be involved in the preparation of food may help them with their eating skills. Preparing food together can be a lot of fun and cooking involves the development of all kinds of skills that may benefit your child, such as number recognition, reading skills, fine motor skills and independence skills.

Melisa Hood offers the following advice:

" *Try to involve your child in the planning and preparation of meals where possible. Let them look through recipe books and choose a meal themselves. Encourage them to get involved in shopping, loading the trolley if possible, ticking off items as they go in, packing, unpacking. In the kitchen try to include them in tasks that they can complete such as washing fruit and vegetables, even cutting them up and putting them in pans. With support they may be able to weigh ingredients, grate cheese, mash potatoes, roll out pastry and tear salad leaves.* **"**

In this chapter we will explore why cooking can help your child to eat and how to motivate your child to be more interested in mealtimes. We will look at shopping trips and how to plan meals involving your child as much as possible. Food hygiene is an important topic that will be explored and suggestions will be given for easy activities that you can try at home.

The positives about cooking

You may be wondering why you should try to encourage your child to engage in cookery activities if they have a food issue, but learning to cook can provide your child with a lot of skills. Even children with profound and multiple learning difficulties can access food preparation and be provided with a multi-sensory experience where they can smell different foods and feel varying textures.

Nicole Freeman, who set up Kids' Kitchen cookery classes for children, explains where her inspiration came from:

" *I've always loved cooking and, after having children, became more aware of how many kids were becoming fussy eaters, eating a lot of pre-prepared fast food. These kids couldn't recognize everyday ingredients. My son was a very fussy eater when he was little and I found that cooking with him and playing games with his food was a great way of encouraging him to try more things. When he started school I thought it was finally time to put into practice some of the ideas I'd had about cooking classes and see what the reaction was from parents and their children. So I started running holiday cooking classes for children back in Summer 2010 and have now expanded to include Sunday morning cooking sessions as well as term-time classes for pre-school children.* "

Nicole firmly believes that encouraging children to cook can help with their eating:

" *It sounds like a cliché, but from my experience, it really is true that children are more likely to try food that they have helped to prepare. At the Kids' Kitchen we really do find that involving the kids in preparing and cooking their own meals encourages them to try new foods.*

Children are always really positive and keen to get stuck in. Whether they are chopping, stirring, or grating, it never ceases to amaze me how much they can do when you give them the chance. Most of my mini-chefs are very independent when cooking, and you can really see their satisfaction as they take home what they have made for their family to try. You'd be surprised how many times mums tell me how impressed they are that their child has tried something in class that they would normally refuse to eat and that they are now clamouring to make that dish at home. And that's something you can replicate at home by cooking regularly with your kids. "

Nicole offers some sensible advice:

" *Do remember that we are encouraging children to try new things and so develop their palate. We aren't trying to force them to like all the new foods they try. As adults we don't all like eating the same things, and there's no reason our children should either! The important thing is that by cooking their own dishes, they are more likely to try a new food. I encourage them to try something before they say they don't like it, but it's ok if they don't like it. And that's why I give certificates in class for trying the new food. This is very motivating for the children. Equally it's really easy to pass on our own food prejudices, so be careful and remember that if you are expecting your child to try something new then you should too! You may be surprised. For example, many kids I see love olives, which are quite an acquired taste, even for many adults.* "

Nicole's classes also cater for children with additional needs and more details can be found about her work at www.thekidskitchen.net.

Do not dismiss the idea of cooking with your child because they have additional needs. You can make cooking accessible for all children in some way. This may be that you allow them to feel the texture of foods prior to and after peeling, for example. Hand on hand support can be offered to allow them to take part in stirring activities or while rolling pastry. Baking is often cheaper and healthier than shop-bought alternatives.

It is highly likely that you will cook on a regular basis and therefore this activity can fit in with your family life relatively easily. Cooking with your child allows them to handle a variety of foods and this can be helpful to introduce them to different foods and textures. Cooking is one of the best ways of teaching your child a range of skills in a fun way. Here are some ways that cooking can help with teaching a range of concepts:

✓ Your child will learn about weights
✓ Following recipes can help with reading skills

✓ You can use words to help your child expand their vocabulary of food items and kitchen equipment

✓ You can explore where food has come from together

✓ Your child may be able to improve motor skills through mixing, chopping, peeling and so on

✓ You can talk about the colours of different foods

✓ Number recognition is an important factor in cookery

✓ Your child can learn about scientific concepts such as melting, and the way foods change when heated or frozen

✓ Your child can improve their social awareness, for example, by making food for parties or sharing food

Why cooking can help

Cooking can help children who have food issues as it can provide them with a real sense of how food is to be enjoyed. If your child enjoys preparing meals, they are more likely to be motivated to try the food offered at mealtimes. Allowing your child to develop a role in the preparation of food can help to boost their self-esteem and allow them to take some ownership of what is happening at mealtimes. Tasks offered need to be appropriate and not put pressure on your child's skills. You must make sure that your child can complete the task and gain some success from their input; cooking should be a positive experience for them.

Nikki Geddes runs www.kiddycook.co.uk and runs cooking classes and workshops for children and young people. She tells us:

❝ *Our classes aim to introduce youngsters to the wonderful world of food. We encourage them to learn about the origins of food and the science behind the cooking. The children don't just bake a cake, they get to create carbon dioxide rockets and bread bubble bombs to show them the chemical reaction that makes their ingredients rise. We also like to give children the opportunity to try ingredients that they may have never tasted before, broadening their food horizons and educating their palette.* **❞**

Nikki goes on to explain:

" *Children are more likely to eat healthy food if they have had a hand in preparing it. If children see their friends eating different foods and if they have helped to prepare a meal we find they are more likely to try it. Cooking is an excellent way to develop self-help skills as well as to build confidence. Children as young as two years old can help out in the kitchen by helping to wash vegetables, for example. If we make preparing and cooking food part of our everyday life children are more likely to want to get involved with the cooking process. Cooking with your child is also a great opportunity to talk and have fun.* **"**

Kiddy Cook is inclusive in its approach and Nikki tells us:

" *We are committed to giving every child the chance to get cooking and develop their skills. We are very flexible in our approach and tailor sessions according to the needs of the individual child or the group. We are currently working alongside a speech and language therapist in order to ensure that our recipe cards are accessible to children with additional needs.* **"**

Julia Wolman is a freelance nutritionist specializing in baby and child nutrition. You can visit her website at www.teenytummies.co.uk. She tells us:

" *It is a well-known strategy that getting children to help with preparing food can make them more inclined to want to eat it. It's not a miracle cure for feeding issues, unfortunately there isn't one, but it can certainly help. Cooking can be exciting and allowing children to get involved without any associated pressure to actually eat anything can help them to feel relaxed around food, which is an essential first step in helping to overcome feeding issues.* **"**

Julia set up Teeny Tummies to provide advice and support to parents on feeding their babies and children. She says:

❝ *Getting children involved in the kitchen doesn't have to mean actual 'cooking' in the traditional sense. It can be any aspect of food preparation. Even simple things like washing fruits and vegetables, spreading a sandwich or laying a table can be really exciting to a child and give them increased confidence around food. I make a lot of soups and smoothies and always make sure that I ask my 3-year-old if he wants to press the button on the hand blender; such a simple thing but he loved doing this and seeing all the ingredients mix together and he loves the noise.* ❞

Julia goes on to explain about the skills that cookery can provide:

❝ *Any of the aspects of cooking discussed can help children to develop their fine motor skills, especially things like spreading and chopping, using a blunt knife, of course! It's important that parents talk to their child about what they're doing, helping them notice the colours and shapes of foods. Taking a moment to talk about and experience the feel and smell of different ingredients can also help to develop sensory skills.* ❞

The aim of encouraging your child to cook is to make the experience enjoyable, Julia reminds us:

❝ *Getting children involved in cooking can help to reduce anxieties that a child might have around food and help them to feel comfortable and relaxed. It's really important that parents remember this and never put any pressure on their child to taste or eat anything if they really don't want to; this will just take away any of the fun aspect and could precipitate feeding issues further. Talking about the colours, smells and how much they are enjoying cooking with their child will all help. Getting creative, like making patterns or smiley faces, for example, with pizzas or sandwiches also makes food fun.* ❞

Sarah teaches in a special school and says:

" *Cookery is a great way of including children in activities; even the children with the most profound learning disabilities can be actively included in cookery sessions. I make sure that everybody has an opportunity to touch the food and to smell the aromas. Tasks have to be matched to abilities but I find with one to one support most children can have a go at chopping vegetables, rolling pastry and icing buns.* "

Choosing recipes

Children love making choices and it is a good idea to encourage them to choose recipes that you can try together. Your child does not have to be able to read the recipes to make a choice. You can show your child a selection of pictures to choose from to find out what they would like to eat. If your child has severe learning difficulties you may wish to make choices very simple, for example, if you are making a milkshake together you could show them some strawberries and a banana and encourage them to touch or eye point to the ingredients that they would like to include in the recipe.

Making choices about what they are preparing will make your child feel more involved in the process. Depending on their skills they may be able to follow a simple recipe. If they have difficulty with reading skills consider whether they would be able to follow picture cues, so, for example, if you take a photograph of a bowl, would they then be able to find the same bowl in your kitchen? While this does take some preparation, laminating the pictures will mean that you create a resource that can be used time and time again.

It is also important that children are encouraged to engage in cooking a range of dishes and not just restricted to cooking cakes and biscuits. Julia Wolman says:

" *Fun cooking doesn't have to be only about cakes and sweets. There are plenty of baking recipes that use fruits and vegetables: banana bread, carrot and courgette muffins, and apple and raisin cupcakes are just a few ideas. A little tip when baking with fruit is to increase the quantity. For example use four bananas if the recipe says three and reduce the quantity of sugar, it always works just fine. Adding ingredients like oats or substituting half white flour for wholemeal can also increase the nutritional value of recipes.* 🍴

Nicole Freeman highlights how easy it can be to make cooking activities fun:

🍴 *Turn cooking into an adventure based around their interests. At The Kids' Kitchen we often theme our classes; this can be a great way of introducing new foods in an entertaining way. At Halloween, for example, we make a green witches' brew. This is basically a fresh fruit smoothie using fresh spinach to make it green. All the kids love it, though many would never ordinarily eat spinach! And we've had great fun cooking football or princess themed goodies.* 🍴

Nicole advises, 'Let them be the chef. Allow your kids to choose a cookery book they like from the bookshop or library and find a recipe that's suitable for dinner. Making them feel in charge of what's made for supper is a fun way of getting them involved and let them help you shop for ingredients.'

There are also many simple children's recipes available online; see Chapter 12 for a list of websites that have great ideas for cooking with your child.

Shopping for ingredients

Shopping trips with children can be difficult at the best of times. It is, however, a good idea to involve them in shopping for the ingredients for the recipes that you have decided to try. This will again give them a feeling of involvement in the whole process. If your child becomes very distressed in large stores you may wish to consider whether shopping at local, smaller stores would be easier or even whether shopping online could be an option, showing your child pictures of food that you could choose. You may want to take your child shopping for food for the recipe they have chosen, outside of the main shopping trip.

Preparing a shopping list is an activity that you can involve your child in. You may wish to keep labels from tins so that your child can be encouraged to look for a label that matches while out and about. Or if your child has good reading skills you could provide them with a written shopping list. Other children may need photographs or pictures to help them to understand what they are looking for while at the shops.

Kelly has a daughter with severe learning difficulties and says:

" *Charlotte used to hate going shopping and I used to find it incredibly difficult to get round the supermarket without her having a meltdown. I started to give her jobs to do in the hope that this would keep her busy and it worked incredibly well. She can't read but she can recognize packages so I save old labels and packages and give her five items to find while we are at the supermarket. I give her lots of prompts when I know we are near the item and make sure that the items are spread throughout the store so that she remains engaged. She is so proud of herself when she finds the food and I give her lots of praise. It has turned shopping trips into a pleasure rather than a pain and has definitely helped with increasing her self-esteem.* "

Kitchen equipment

You do not need to buy any special kitchen equipment for your child but sometimes it can be helpful for them to have something of their own to make them feel special and involved. This will depend on your child but may be an item like a special apron or a chef's hat. Perhaps you have a small wooden spoon that you could write their name on or draw a smiley face on so they know which spoon to find to help with stirring. Involve them in the choosing of the item; many items can be printed with children's names and this can help them to develop a sense of ownership.

Food hygiene

While we aim for cookery sessions to be fun it is also important that hygienic practice in the kitchen is adhered to. Children need to be taught good practice from the beginning and the simplest skill is to learn that it is essential to wash their hands before preparing food to avoid the spread of bacteria. This can be a difficult concept for children to understand because bacteria can't be seen.

Begin each cookery session by washing hands using soap and warm water. Make sure that you encourage your child to wash their hands throughout cookery activities. If they need prompting on how to do this you can make a visual timetable by taking photographs of the activity and breaking it down into stages. For example, your first photograph may be turning on the tap, the second putting their hands in the water, the third applying the soap and so on. Ensure that your child has their sleeves rolled up and is wearing an apron. Long hair should be tied up.

Easy to follow activities

It is important that initially you begin by introducing simple cookery activities that your child will find easy to follow and get quick results from. Here are some examples of simple tasks that you can do with your child to ignite their interest in cooking:

✓ Buy pizza bases ready-made and encourage your child to add ingredients for the topping. You could get them to make patterns or smiley faces

✓ Get your child to decorate a biscuit. A packet of plain biscuits is ideal to provide the base, then use icing sugar to stick on a variety of fruit or sweets

✓ Smoothies are easy to make. Simply put two cups of milk and your fruit in a blender with half a cup of natural yoghurt and around six ice cubes. Mix it all up and there you have a perfect smoothie. Experiment with adding in different flavoured fruit, a spoonful of honey or a flavoured yoghurt

✓ Milkshakes are also good to try. Add four scoops of ice cream, half a cup of milk and whichever fruit you prefer. Mix it all up and taste! If you want the shake to be thicker then add less milk and more ice cream

✓ Use shaped cutters so that sandwich-making is far more fun

✓ Experiment with making different drinks by adding different fruit juices; you can decorate the glass with a cocktail umbrella and give them fancy names

✓ Let them make their own ice lollies; you can buy moulds that go into the freezer. Simply fill with their favourite fruit juice: you could even add chunks of real fruit

Nicole Freeman suggests getting creative to help support your child's eating:

" *Play games with food. For example, if I'm trying to encourage kids to eat small fruit like grapes, blueberries or raisins, I will make it into a game, encouraging the kids to pick up the fruit from a small plastic bowl with a toothpick (this is good for developing fine motor skills) and then upturning the bowl on their head like a hat when they've finished. We've also bobbed for apples, bitten dried apple and pineapple from bits of string that I've held in the air, no hands allowed, 'painted' our lips with beetroot and then made beetroot prints on paper, munched fruit slices; banana, oranges, pineapple etc, into different shapes using our 'mouth scissors', which to grown-ups inter- prets as 'teeth'. The list is endless!*

Fruit smoothies are a great way of using up fruit and encouraging your kids to try something new as they won't taste an ingredient they might not like when it's combined with lots of others. Similarly, blitz fruits of a similar colour – berries are great here, or apricots, mangoes and peaches – to make a 'sauce' and then get your kids to try 'painting' with yoghurt. Blend in the red or orange sauce and see what swirly patterns and colours they get. You can also use the sauce to make an ice-cream sundae. Put in some crushed biscuits or meringues and you have a quick, simple and tasty dessert with some hidden fruit. **"**

Photographing finished products

Everybody loves to feel that what they have produced has been valued. Why not photograph your child with their finished product and start a scrapbook? Children tend to love looking at photographs of themselves and this would allow them a pictorial record of their activities in the kitchen. It will also act as a reminder of all the wonderful things you have made together.

Cooking for a purpose

It is helpful if you can create a purpose for your child's cooking. This can help them to feel more motivated to be involved and instil a sense of pride in the finished product. Ideas for cooking for a purpose may include:

✓ Inviting a friend to tea
✓ Making a gift for a teacher, such as a cupcake
✓ Preparing a birthday cake for a family member
✓ To provide items for their own packed lunch
✓ Making food items to share at school (check the school's policy on this first)
✓ Making items for charity events such as cake stalls at village fairs
✓ Preparing a picnic
✓ Cooking for celebrations such as Christmas, Diwali or Chinese New Year

In summary

Cooking can be an enjoyable activity and may also help your child with their eating issues. The experience should always be a positive one for both you and your child so you may wish to begin gradually by encouraging your child to help you by using an appliance, for example, where they see a quick result. Lots of verbal praise should be given for your child's efforts.

Nicole Freeman tells us:

" *Cooking is a fun activity that you can easily share with your child at home by setting aside some time each week. I believe that if kids enjoy their time in the kitchen it will lay the foundation for a love of cooking and a curiosity about food and where it comes from. And this is of great benefit for them as individuals as well as for the wider family; cooking new recipes together can be as much of a learning experience for parents as for children.* "

Chapter 11
How to Help Children with Special Needs or Eating Issues Take Medication

If your child has additional needs, they may need to take medication on an occasional or regular basis. This can be fraught with difficulties. You child may know and dislike the medication, or simply be averse to anything new and strange going in their mouth. Whatever the reason, as a parent you are under pressure to succeed and deliver the medication that your child needs. Read this chapter for tips and hints on how to do it, and to discover other parents' experiences.

Why children won't take medicine

Before you even start to offer you child their medicine, it will help to understand why they might be rejecting it.

Depending on their level of understanding, it can be hard for a child to appreciate why they need medication at all. It can make them feel different from their friends or siblings. Younger children copy what their parents do too – have they ever seen you taking medicine?

If your child already uses food as a way of exerting control over a situation (see Chapter 4) they may do the same with medicine. They will be able to see the range of emotions you express as they refuse, and feel that they have some power. Being ill and under the care of doctors can make anyone, adult or child, feel disempowered, and refusing to co-operate can give your child the control they feel they need.

Many medications just don't taste great. When faced with something unfamiliar that might taste bad, children tend to refuse. If they have regular medication that they know tastes bad refusal becomes very likely. With chronic conditions that require regular medication your child may be well aware of the side effects they are likely to experience and reject medication for this reason. If your child has had side effects from some medication in the past they will remember this and possibly have concerns about taking any new medication in the future, whether side effects are likely or not.

Tablets can cause children difficulty too: few children find them easy to swallow, and a dislike of the form in which the medication is presented can lead to refusal.

The importance of taking prescribed medicine

If your child is prescribed medication, as a parent you are very aware of the importance of getting them to take it. Pharmacist Sarah Newbury says:

❝ *Compliance with prescribed medication, either for a short course of antibiotics or long-term treatment can be difficult for anyone but if the patient is a child or person with special needs, then a whole different range of challenges must be met. Many issues with medicating a young person stem from problems with swallowing tablets or capsules whole. This is not some-thing young children are familiar, or comfortable, with. Indeed, swallowing anything at all may be an issue for children or young people with special needs. Compliance is paramount to ensuring the patient gets the right quantity or the right dose of medication every time.* ❞

Helping your child

The first step to helping your child is to think about your own attitude. Sian's son has been taking his medications six times a day since he was about three months old. She says:

❝ *I think that if a child requires long-term medication the most useful, sensible and logical thing to do is to administer it in a normal, non-fussy way. After all, the child has a condition which requires treatment, this is normal for them and the medication should be built into their day as a normal and routine, non-special, matter of course. The maintenance of this condition (meds, physio etc.) should be normalized as much as possible for the sake of the child's emotional well-being and self-esteem.*

Taking medications is as normal to my son as brushing his teeth. Thankfully he likes his medication and he understands fully why he has to take it and why he has to take it so often. Because of this he is a more compliant patient and his treatment has been as effective as it could possibly have been and I do not worry when he is away from me or when he grows up that he won't know how to manage his medications; I have enabled him to do that already and that's what parents need to do. But that's just my view. I know some people mix the medication he takes into squash, apple sauce or yoghurt. **"**

As a parent you need to watch how you react when you give your child their meds. If you feel bad, try not to let it show. Instead, be matter of fact, as Sarah suggests above, making it normal. If you pull a face, your child will know that something bad is coming.

To help your child take their meds, make sure it happens at the same time every day. Children like routine. Approach your child gently but firmly when it is medication time. Don't offer an option: 'Would you like your medicine?' Instead, offer a choice where they can feel in control: 'Would you like chocolate or strawberry milk-shake to wash your tablets down?'

As we have discussed in earlier chapters, mealtimes can become a stress point when your child battles against you, and the same is true for taking medications. If you have a daily battle with your child over medication, think what you can do to break the pattern. Take a deep breath or count to ten if you feel you are getting stressed or angry. See if you can take turns with another adult to do the meds. Try to avoid forcing your child to take medication, and don't make it seem like a punishment. Read the tips below for lots of strategies and ideas to help you and your child make medication time a positive experience. Don't worry if sometimes the tips don't work for you. Do ask for help from your child's doctor, pharmacist, or the SENCO at school.

Annabel says, 'Don't be afraid to ask the doctors questions or to try to find other parents dealing with the same medical conditions and medications. We've had so many different suggestions provided to us just by being able to talk to other parents dealing with JIA (Oglioarticular Juvenile Idiopathic Arthritis) that we're hoping something might work.'

Medication challenges

If your child is able to verbalize their feelings, ask them what they dislike about their medication and you will be one step closer to addressing their concerns. If your child can't tell you, you may need to do some detective work.

Some children don't understand why they need medication. Depending on your child's level of understanding, a simple explanation or discussion about how the medication helps can motivate them to take it. If you have an older child, ask the doctor to explain how the medication helps. Tie your explanations in to what motivates your child. If they have been complaining about pain, explain that the medication helps the pain. If your child has medication for ADHD, explain how it might help them make friends, or concentrate on their work and get praise from teachers. For younger children and those with cognitive issues, act out helping a toy by giving it medication. When your child's condition begins to improve praise them for looking after themselves and taking their medication.

Tackling tablets

Swallowing a tablet can be a big deal for a child. It takes a certain amount of development to have sufficient control over swallowing. Some children can swallow tablets aged three or four, while others struggle into their teens.

Tablets can feel uncomfortable as they go down. Reassure your child that practising will help. Offer a drink to help the tablet go down: a milkshake or other thick drink can help smooth the passage of the tablet.

Some tablets can be cut in half: a smaller tablet will always be easier to swallow so ask your pharmacist for advice. Tablet cutters are available. Pharmacist Sarah Newbury advises:

“ *It is important that the parent/carer checks with their doctor or pharmacist first. Whether or not tablets can be crushed will depend on the tablet. In many cases, it will be fine but, as always, there are exceptions. Certain medications have special 'enteric coatings' (EC), which allow the tablets to be absorbed further down the oesophagus to protect the stomach lining. Other medications will be 'slow release' (SR), or 'modified release' (MR), and will be adversely affected by being cut. So, crushing a tablet to aid administration can destroy its pharmacokinetic properties. In this case, an alternative dosage form to a tablet would need to be considered. The most obvious one of these, for a child using the oral route, would be a liquid (syrup or suspension).* ”

Do mention to your doctor at the time of prescribing if your child would prefer liquid medication. Sarah explains:

“ *For example, Phenytoin for epilepsy is available as a capsule, chew tab or liquid. Liquid preparations are easier to swallow but do have their own problems, namely texture and taste. Liquid preparations, such as antibiotics, are usually formulated to have a pleasant taste and different manufacturers use different flavourings so it's worth checking at the pharmacy before the prescription is made up. This, however, is not the case with all liquids. A caution for liquids is that you cannot assume all of them will be formulated suitably for children, or that all drugs are stable in liquid form. Also, certain excipients are added to liquids to extend their shelf life and some of these can be alcohol-based. The doctor and pharmacist will check this but if the liquid the patient requires is not available 'off the shelf', most pharmacies can organize for a formulation (be it sugar-free, alcohol-free or preservative-free) to be made up specially. The downside to this is that it will need to be ordered, may take time to reach the pharmacy and, without a preservative, won't last longer than four weeks or so. This means many regular trips to the pharmacy for Mum!* ”

Talk to the pharmacist to see whether the tablets come in round or oval shapes, as ovals can be easier to swallow. Some capsule medications can be opened and sprinkled onto a spoonful of food. Remember, do always seek advice before cutting up or opening medication as this can affect the way the drug is released.

Taste tips

There are no two ways about it: many medications taste bad. If your child has bitter tablets, offer a favourite flavoured drink to help wash them down. Alternatively, follow up with a spoonful of a favourite food. Some parents crush medication into food. Do tell your child what you are doing, as this can help them understand that they are taking medication and realize that it is necessary for their health. Equally, you'll need to ensure that all the food is finished so your child gets a full dose.

Some medications come in a choice of flavours. Take a few moments to ask the pharmacist about whether there are options for flavouring. Sarah Newbury advises:

" *Palatability is an important factor in compliance with long-term, regular medication but not all liquids are formulated with children's taste buds in mind and not all children will agree on what's nice and what's not! Many parents will have tried to mask unpleasant-tasting medicines in sweet-tasting spoonfuls of honey, apple sauce or jam. Again, I would recommend speaking to the doctor or pharmacist first to check that there are no incompatibilities between the food/drink and the medication.* **"**

Should I hide my child's medication in food?

Most parents have wondered whether to disguise medication. Sarah Newbury says:

" *If you are going to hide medication in your child's food, the food ideally should be soft: for example, yoghurts, soft cheese,*

Food and Your Special Needs Child

apple sauce and jam or honey, as mentioned previously. The sweetness of these can mask the taste of the medicine. Children with autism are often required to take vitamin supplements which can be administered using fizzy powder to mask the flavour. Whatever you choose to try, I would advise that the smallest amount of food or drink be used to prevent problems with dosage if the child doesn't eat or drink the whole amount the medication is hidden in. The main issue with hiding medication in food is that problems may arise if the child develops an aversion or dislike for that food. You then have to move on to something else. This itself may be a concern for those on a limited or restricted diet. 〝

See Chapter 4 for more about the issues of disguised food.

Different delivery

Some parents have had success by delivering medication in a different way. Some toddlers like medication from a dropper in preference to a spoon. Helen says, 'In the past, when one child has had measured lemon yellow antibiotics from a syringe, I've had to give the other one a squirt of custard from a similar syringe. They think it is a fun way to take medicine.' Your pharmacist may also be able to supply a small measuring cup.

One clever trick is to aim medication from the syringe further back in the mouth or inside the cheek to avoid the taste buds.

Facing refusals

Many parents want to know what to do if their child spits or dribbles some of the medication. Sarah Newbury advises:

〝 *If a particular flavour or texture is initially accepted by the child and then spat or dribbled out or, indeed, if the food or drink the medicine has been disguised in hasn't been finished, it becomes difficult to know just how much of the dose has been ingested. It has been suggested that if the child spits out or vomits within thirty minutes of a dose, or seems to have spat out a significant amount of the original dose, then the whole dose can be repeated. I must emphasize again here the importance of using the smallest possible amount of food/drink to hide the medication in so you can tell if it has been consumed. Giving the child a drink after their medication may help to ensure the dose has gone down. For younger children or those with special needs, a plastic 'pelican bib' could be used to catch any spat out or dribbled medicine. This could then be re-administered if suitable.* "

What if a child misses a dose or simply will not take it?

Realistically, you may miss a dose of medication. In this situation Sarah Newbury advises:

" *With once-daily doses, the missed dose should be given as soon as remembered within the same day but double doses should not be administered the following day if not remembered until then. If a child simply refuses to take the dose, then walk away from the situation and try again in half an hour. Try to keep calm. You don't want to get angry or make taking medicine seem like a punishment. You should not force the child but try explaining why they must take it and praise the child when any improvement is seen.* "

Treat time?

If your child only has medication on an occasional basis, a treat can help. Stickers, stars, sweets – parents have tried all sorts of things to get children to take their medicine, but this can become impractical if your child has medication in the long term.

Annabel's daughter Erin has recently been diagnosed with Extended Oglioarticular Juvenile Idiopathic Arthritis. The condition has initially been controlled by giving steroid injections into the joints under a general anaesthetic. Erin has also had oral steroids and is now on long-term medication, Methotrexate. Annabel says:

" *This week she has also started to take folic acid and an anti-sickness medication to help control some of the side effects of the Methotrexate. Methotrexate is very bitter, so Erin doesn't like the taste. It can also make the child feel nauseous, and have sleep disturbances, which then cause them to feel tired, which Erin suffers from. Erin has a severe needle phobia so we aren't able to give her the Methotrexate in its usual form, which is by injection. Instead, she is given it in a liquid form orally, which we administer by syringe. We have had Erin scream, cry, hide, try to run away out of the front door, cover her mouth, go into hysterics and be so anxious and upset about it that after having half a dose she vomits. Due to her anxieties and experiences with taking the Methotrexate, when we tried to administer the folic acid this week – again in liquid form – she had a meltdown and it took a lot of convincing to get her to overcome her fear of it tasting awful and making her feel sick. We did research the medication when Erin was first diagnosed with JIA, so we weren't totally surprised with any side effects etc. There were a couple of times when we were first starting the medication where Erin spat the medication out, threw it up, we spilled it etc., and we were quite worried and concerned that she hadn't received the full dose, when in fact it's no big deal if that happens every now and again. We are far more relaxed about it now if it does happen.* **"**

Annabel has tried all sorts of strategies to help her daughter with the medication. She says:

" *At first Erin was okay taking the medication, but she soon decided she didn't like it or how it made her feel. We sought advice from the doctor and they said we could hide it in drinks, reward her, whatever it took to get it into her. When she started not to want to take the medication we tried to hide it in her drinks, but she could still taste it. It could take up to an hour to get her to take a 5 ml dose of the medication. We then started* *to allow her to choose a special drink, a smoothie or Fruit Shoot, each week when she had to have her medication. She would take a big drink, have half a dose, take another big drink, and have the other half. Again, this didn't work for very long on its own. The next thing was to give her a reward every four weeks if she took her medication without fussing. This worked for about three months, but then we had to start rewarding her every two weeks as she really didn't want to take her meds. The day she tried to run out of the front door to run away from her medication we changed tactics again! We started to get the reward ahead of time, have it on display for when she was having the medication and, if she was good every two weeks, she got the reward. Now she sometimes gets a reward every two weeks or she gets something every week (depends on what the reward is and the cost). The reward can be as simple as a packet of crisps (she isn't allowed crisps very much), or a coin for her Innotab, a toy, a magazine, etc. This, of course, could mount up as she could be on this medication for up to two years – or longer, depending on how she does with it. Whenever Erin has her medication, she is cuddled either by myself or her father. It helps to restrain her gently and hold her in place. If she isn't feeling very well to start with, the job of getting her to take her medication is harder, so we are still looking for ways to continue to improve it.* **""**

For children who take medication over the long term you need to devise your reward strategy carefully. Sian says:

"" *If you get into a situation where medications require a performance or special treatment then changes to the medication present a bit of a difficulty; if a child expects a Mars bar when he/she has medication once a day and it suddenly goes up to three or four times, you cannot deny the child the expected Mars bars as you have led them to that expectation. Tantrums will ensue.* **""**

When all else fails

There is an enormous amount of pressure on parents to ensure their children take their medications. Sometimes all the tips and tricks still don't work, and your child will continue to resist. If your child has to take medication on a long-term basis, and is struggling, ask your consultant for support or a specialist referral. Annabel says:

" We are having play therapy to deal with Erin's severe anxieties and phobias with regards to treatments and needles. While taking the medication, Erin requires blood tests every three months to ensure that her liver is still functioning normally, and that her white blood cells, platelets and red blood cells are fine, as the medication can cause issues with all of them. We have had help from the pain management team who provide us with play therapy, and from the rheumatology nurse specialist with ideas as to how to give Erin the medication and things they have heard from other parents over the years. We know that, if we struggle with getting Erin to take her medication in liquid form, we can go to them and they will try it in tablet form, if that is available. The pain management team and psychology department are also working with us to help get Erin's anxieties and phobias under control in case we do need to move to injection-form medication. The therapy has been mainly focused on getting her to be able to deal with her anxiety and phobia about needles, and less on the medication. It is something we will be bringing up with the pain management team when our sessions start again as it may well help Erin and make it much easier to give her the medications. "

Taking medicine at school

Taking medication at school can be an issue. Not every child is keen to take their medication at school. Some struggle with being different, and resent having to take time out for medication. They may be concerned about bullying. Unless the school co-operates, it can be easy for a child to forget to take their medication.

Sian has had serious issues with support from the school. She says:

" *After my son was offered a place and I accepted I wrote the school a letter describing his medical conditions, medications and what they need to do in case of emergencies. I then spoke to the class teacher, the SENCO and the school nurse to draw up a care plan. The arrangement was that he should go to the office to take the medication at the correct time; the teacher was to set an alarm in the classroom. All was fine (a few hiccups but nothing major) until the class teacher was sick and they were sent to different classrooms and the teachers has not seen his care plan and he missed all of his medications. Nobody told me; it was not until much later that my son mentioned that he had a supply teacher so I asked and he said he hadn't taken them. I was annoyed as he takes another medication in the evening which must be balanced with his daily one or it can cause skeletal phosphate leaking. I spoke to the teacher and SENCO who were apologetic and they said that the care plan should have been consulted.*

A little while later they had another supply teacher. He hadn't taken his medication all day but was told in the afternoon, before school pick-up, to go to the office and take all three doses that he had missed. All at once. I was fuming at this because he already has compromised kidney function and though the meds aren't toxic at that dosage (though they couldn't know that) this overdose would have exacerbated it. I went directly to the headmaster and asked why the care plan was again not consulted by the supply teacher and I quite calmly explained my dismay to him. He said he would look into it. He looked into it and then informed me that the school were not happy to accept any responsibility at all for his meds. Even though they were in loco parentis they did not feel obliged to help him take his meds. They insisted I would have to attend for each of his three doses during the school day to give him his medications. At that time I was recovering from major surgery, in a lot of pain and unable to walk to and from the school eight times a day and thought it was unreasonable, especially as he would not allow my son to wear a watch in class so as to remember the medication himself.

The headmaster wanted access to my son's medical records to see why he needed the medication. I told him that was inappropriate and he must respect my son's right to confidentiality but I would provide a letter from the hospital. I had to remove my son from school until we sorted it out as I couldn't be sure they would look after him fully. Needless to say, I had no confidence in the school and all goodwill and trust were eroded by their handling of the situation.

We moved schools to a small, one-form entry primary school. The teaching has been consistent and the teachers and admin staff know him well. He now brings his medicine mixed in a plastic bottle, wears a watch with an alarm set for every two hours and goes to the office to take his medicine at the appropriate time. Occasionally he misses a dose but they know to just carry on and will tell me or he will tell me so that he doesn't take too much of the other medicine. The office staff have even texted me to tell me he has missed one if he goes to after-school club. He went on a week-long residential course and they were utterly inclusive and made no issue of it at all. That's how it should be. They facilitate and support him in taking his medicines as best they can and will even administer painkillers and antibiotics if necessary. I should mention that his school is remarkably small; there are only twenty children in the class with a teacher and a full-time TA, the admin staff have not changed and he has had the same TA for two years so they all know him personally and are familiar with his medical conditions. I don't think he has ever had a supply teacher in the four years he has been there so I would say that turnover and consistency of staff is very important. As with all children but especially for those who need extra support, school should be a nurturing and supportive environment. Working with the school, and talking to the SENCO and school nurse to draw up a care plan and all that stuff will only work if the people implementing it care. 🔴

If you have worries about your child taking medicine at school, here are some steps to take. Start by talking to the teacher about your concerns. If your child is embarrassed, ask for help finding a time and place where your child can have their medication in private. The teacher may have a chat in class about 'being different' and help all the class understand that people can vary in many ways.

Sarah Newbury advises, 'If your child needs medication during school time, there should be someone available to administer or oversee the administering of the dose. If the school/teacher is reluctant, try discussing it with them to come up with an agreement that causes fewest problems for your child.'

For children who forget to take their medication, a watch with an alarm like Sian's son's may help. Back this up with support from an adult at school: this can be easier in primary school where your child has one teacher for most lessons. In secondary school there may be help available from the support staff. Discuss with the doctor who prescribed the medication what your child should do if they miss a dose as this will vary depending on what they are prescribed. Let the school know what should happen in this event.

If your child struggles with taking medication at school it may be possible to adjust how and when they take their drugs. Ask your doctor or pharmacist for advice on when to take medication to avoid a school-time dose. Sarah Newbury says:

66 *Another option may be to see if a slow-release form of the medication is available. For example, children on methylphenidate could try the slow-release tablets Concerta XL or Equasym XL. This would allow a once-a-day dose to be given in the morning before school. This dose would be released slowly throughout the day without the child having to worry about a dose during school hours.* 99

Getting your child to take their prescribed medication can be a battle, but it is important for children to get the doses of medication they need for therapeutic effect. Sarah Newbury says:

" *Depending on the age, and understanding of the child, it may be worth talking with them to tell them why they need to take the medicine. Maybe the child is worried about being teased or feeling different to other children. Maybe they don't like a side effect or maybe they want to gain back control from doctors and parents, so put up a fight. Or maybe it just tastes horrid. Whatever it is, listen to their concerns. Communicate with them as best you can and together, solutions can be found. Always be firm and fair.*

I've mentioned previously some tips to help children to swallow their medicines. Here are a few more suggestions for parents.

✓ *Stay calm and in control. Take a break if necessary after refusal before trying again*

✓ *Try to make it part of the daily routine. Use the same time each day. Children thrive on routine. They know what to expect when and there are no nasty surprises*

✓ *Instead of saying to the child, 'Time for your medicine' (to which the child may argue), try letting them think they are in charge by saying, 'Do you want to take your tablet with strawberry or raspberry jam today?'*

✓ *Build self-esteem by praising the child whenever possible*

✓ *Do not pretend tablets are sweets. Avoid this association for obvious reasons*

✓ *The parent/carer could pretend to take a tablet at the same time as the child takes theirs*

Always remember, what works well for one child doesn't always work well for another. Keep trying. Do not despair. If none of the strategies work for your child, you can always go back to the doctor or pharmacist or other support worker for help and advice. "

In summary

There are many issues surrounding getting your child to take medication successfully. If this is a challenge in your family, first think about why your child objects. Work out which strategies might match up and meet their concerns. Stay calm, and call in help if you need it. Simply having another adult share the task of giving medication will help you.

Sarah Newbury advises:

66 *Getting a prescription for a medication is often just the start. Getting it inside the reluctant patient is another thing entirely! Here are a few tips:*

- ✓ *Consider your choice of dosage form. Use liquids rather than tablets, if possible, with child-friendly flavour*
- ✓ *Crush tablets/open capsules (after first checking with doctor or pharmacist), and disguise in food/drink if necessary*
- ✓ *Use an oral syringe rather than a spoon to prevent spillages. Direct syringe to inside of cheek rather than to back of throat to prevent choking or spitting back out*
- ✓ *Toddlers may respond well to reward charts or stickers*
- ✓ *Carbonated drinks may help the medicine go down as they 'tickle' the throat thus disguising the feel of the tablet*
- ✓ *Taking a sip of the child's favourite drink before popping the tablet in and swallowing helps the tablet float and not touch the tongue or throat*
- ✓ *A sweet treat after the medication has gone down helps to take away any nasty flavours left in the mouth* 99

Beyond these tips, speak to your child's GP or consultant about further help. Your pharmacist may also have good ideas on how to help your child take their medication.

Chapter 12
Healthy Eating Resources

As a parent, some of the first healthy eating advice you get could be from your health visitor. A health visitor is a nurse or midwife with additional training who works with families in the community to promote health and well-being. If you need more help with healthy eating, ask your GP for a referral to a dietician, or the health visitor may be able to make the referral.

According to the Health Professions Council who regulate dieticians, 'a dietitian uses the science of nutrition to devise eating plans for patients to treat medical conditions. They promote good health by helping to facilitate a positive change in food choice'.

Find out more about dieticians from the British Dietetic Society, www.bda.uk.com. The BDA also offers healthy eating, medical condition and allergy fact sheets to download at *www.*bda.uk.com /foodfacts/index.html.

If you can't get a referral via your GP or would prefer to go privately, visit the freelance dieticians site, www.freelancedieticians.org, which offers contact details for registered dieticians who you can consult privately.

There is more advice on choosing a dietician at the NHS choices website, www.nhs.uk. The site also has lot of advice on healthy eating, a meal planner and other tools. Also visit www.nhs.uk/Change4Life for healthy lifestyle advice for all the family.

Resources for when eating goes wrong

If your child has health issues, the first port of call is usually your GP. The GP may make a referral to a paediatrician. A paediatrician is a consultant doctor with expertise in child health issues. The paediatrician will assess your child's health as a whole, but can also help to provide solutions to dietary issues.

There may be a specialist team for your child's condition, such as a dysphagia specialist team or eating disorder clinic: you might need to travel to access such a service. Feeding and Swallowing Advice Clinics are available in different forms across the UK. Speak to your GP or consultant about whether a specialist service would help your child, and to get a referral.

Your child may benefit from seeing an occupational therapist. An occupational therapist uses specific activities to limit the effects of disability and promote independence in all aspects of daily life. They may have tips to help your child with eating at home and school.

If you wish to use a private occupational therapist you can find an online directory using this link www.cot.co.uk/find-ot/find-occupational-therapist. All therapists listed are fully qualified and listed with the Health Care Professionals Council.

The development of the mouth has a big effect on how we eat. If control over the mouth and swallowing is an issue for your child a speech and language therapist can help. A speech and language therapist not only assesses, treats and helps to prevent speech and language issues but will also have a good working knowledge of how the mouth and jaw function and will be able to advise on feeding issues and swallowing difficulties. Speech and language therapy is available on the NHS but if you wish to use a private therapist you can find a list of practitioners by visiting www.helpwithtalking.com.

Physiotherapists deal with human function and movement and help people to achieve their full physical potential. They use physical approaches to promote, maintain and restore well-being. If your child has developmental delays or problems with gross motor co-ordination a physiotherapist can help: improving your child's posture and how they sit, for example, can have benefits for eating and digestion. The Chartered Society for Physiotherapy has a facility to search for a private physiotherapist at www.csp.org.uk.

Eating difficulties may result in poor dental hygiene management or toothache. Build a good relationship with a child-friendly dentist. Visit www.nhs.uk/servicedirectories to find a local dentist.

Some eating issues are down to psychological problems. Clinical psychology aims to reduce psychological distress and to enhance and promote psychological well-being. A clinical psychologist deals with a wide range of psychological difficulties, including anxiety, depression, relationship problems, learning disabilities, child and family problems and serious mental illness. A clinical psychologist will undertake a clinical assessment using a variety of methods including psychological tests, interviews and direct observation of behaviour. Assessment may lead to therapy, counselling or advice. Find a psychologist at www.bps.org.uk.

Psychiatry is a medical field concerned with the diagnosis, treatment and prevention of mental health conditions. A doctor who works in psychiatry is called a psychiatrist. Unlike other mental health professionals, such as psychologists and counsellors, psychiatrists must be medically qualified doctors who have chosen to specialize in psychiatry. This means that they can prescribe medication as well as recommend other forms of treatment. Speak to your GP or specialist if you feel that your child would benefit from referral to a psychiatrist.

Support resources for you

If you feel that you need somebody to talk to you may wish to think about one to one or couples' counselling. Your GP is able to make a referral if necessary or you can contact a private counsellor, however, a fee would be involved.

You may also wish to explore Relate for Parents and Families which is a website that offers support and access to online chat with a Relate counsellor. For more information about this service log on to www.relateforparents.org.uk.

Face 2 Face is a befriending service for parents of children with additional needs. It is managed by Scope and offers emotional support. To find out more about the service log on to the website at www.scope.org.uk.

Parent Partnership services offer information, advice and support to parents and carers of children with special educational needs. Their role is to support parents in having their views understood and you may be offered support when attending meetings. The Parent Partnership service is a voluntary organization and provides confidential and impartial advice. To find out more about their role and to locate your nearest service log on to www.parentpartnership.org.uk.

PINNT is a support group for those receiving artificial nutrition.

The site aims to promote greater understanding of therapies and to provide contact between users. Visit the website at www.pinnt.com.

Support resources for the family

Sibs is a UK charity that is set up to support the needs of those growing up with a brother or sister with additional needs. Their website is packed full of useful information about how to support siblings through difficult times: log on to www.sibs.org.uk.

Contact a Family supports families of children with a disability. They offer a range of services including a helpline, advice about education and support around medical issues. You can log on to their website at www.cafamily.org.uk.

Caudwell Children's Family Support Service provides emotional and emergency practical support to disabled young people and their families from birth, diagnosis or at times of crisis. Visit their website at www.caudwellchildren.com.

Specialist equipment

If you need specialist equipment and it is recommended by a professional, ask first if it can be supplied on the NHS. If that is not an option, the internet has made it much easier to shop around for resources such as:

✓ Drinking cups in easy to use designs
✓ Larger size bibs and washable absorbent bandannas
✓ Easy-grip utensils
✓ Non-slip trays
✓ Rimmed plates
✓ Stay-warm plates
✓ Non-slip plates

You'll find lots of useful resources in the Fledglings catalogue. Fledglings is a national charity that aims to improve the lives of disabled children, and give relief to their carers by supplying through one source a range of products and services to meet individual needs. The products they sell are not priced for profit – the charity makes about a third of the income needed to operate from trading activity. It also provides a helpline, a regular e-newsletter and a product search and development service – all free of charge and funded by grants and donations. Find out more about the charity and its services at www.fledglings.org.uk or read the catalogue: www.fledglings.org.uk/docs/pdf/brochure.pdf. Rackety's (www.disabled-clothing.co.uk) also offers children's and adult bibs and bandannas. Bibs and bandannas are also available from Beauty and the Bib, www.beautyandthebib.com and Dribble Bandanas, www.dribble-bandanas.co.uk. Do not forget to check out eBay and Amazon as many products are now also available on these sites.

Children's medical jewellery can be found at www.icegems.co.uk with prices including free engraving and a medical ID card.

Funding

The Family Fund offers grants to families of children with disabilities who are on a low income. They aim to ease the additional pressures that families face. They help to fund essential items such as washing machines, fridges or even a short break away. To find out about their criteria visit www.familyfund.org.uk.

Relaxation resources

Relax Kids has developed a range of products to encourage children to relax and to ease anxiety. It has a number of relaxation CDs ranging from material suitable for pre-school children to material suitable for teens. It also produces books that you can share with your child and experience guided imagery together to aid their relaxation.

Stories can be useful to help children to normalize their emotions. Below are some examples of story books that you may wish to explore. They are all available from Amazon.

- Virginia Ironside and Frank Rodgers, *The Huge Bag of Worries* (Hodder Children's Books, 2004)
- Elaine Whitehouse and Warwick Pudney, *A Volcano in My Tummy: Helping Children to Handle Anger: a Resource Book for Parents,*

Caregivers and Teachers (New Society Publishers, 1997)
- Hannah Cumming *The Cloud* (Child's Play, 2010)
- Kari Dunn Buron, *When My Worries Get Too Big!: A Relaxation Book for Children Who Live with Anxiety* (Autism Asperger Publishing Co., 2006)
- Amy V. Jaffe and Luci Gardner, *My Book Full of Feelings: How to Control and React to the Size of Your Emotions* (Autism Asperger Publishing Co., 2006)
- Dawn Huebner and Bonnie Matthews, *What to Do When You Worry Too Much: A Kid's Guide to Overcoming Anxiety* (Magination Press, 2005)

Cooking together resources

- Find healthy recipes at www.nhs.uk/Change4Life/Pages/healthy-eating.aspx
- Find child-friendly recipes on the CBeebies website, in the Make and Colour section, www.bbc.co.uk/cbeebies/makes
- Netmums downloadable shopping list to print off that outlines the additives to avoid. Visit www.netmums.com and search for 'food additives'.

Food diaries

This is an example of a food diary, which you can use to track your child's diet. Getting an overview of what they eat, and when, can help professionals work out the best way to deal with any issues.

✓ Complete the diary in as much detail as possible
✓ Share the diary with medical practitioners
✓ Use the diary to identify any food types that your child may be missing out on e.g. proteins, fats, etc.
✓ Remember to complete the diary consistently so that you get an accurate picture of what your child is eating
✓ Ask school to complete a diary so that you can see what your child eats during the day

Meal	Food type	Quantity eaten	Drinks (amount and time)
Breakfast			
Lunch			
Dinner			
Supper			
Any Snacks			

Social Stories

A Social Story may be useful in supporting your child's understanding of dining out and mealtimes. A Social Story describes a situation and shares accurate information so as to enhance understanding of events. They can be particularly useful for children who have difficulty understanding social interaction and are frequently used with children who are on the autism spectrum. You can read more about Social Stories by visiting www.thegraycenter.org. You can buy Social Stories books too (see below).

- Carol Gray, *The New Social Story Book* (Future Horizons Incorporated, 2010)
- Carol Gray (author) and Sean McAndrew (illustrator), *My Social Stories Book* (Jessica Kingsley Publishers, 2001)

Medication resources

Ask your pharmacist for help if you are struggling to get your child to take tablets or medication. A pharmacist will have access to different spoons, cups and syringes to make it easier for your child to take medication, and the pharmacy may also hold a range of catalogues offering helpful products such as tablet cutters and crushers. You can also search online for websites such as www.tabtime.com that offer helpful resources and compare prices of such products on Amazon or eBay. Search on terms such as 'medicine dispenser' to see what is on offer.

If your child takes a range of tablets there are organizers available to set out each day's doses.

Professional bodies and specialist groups

If you are unsure as to whether your child's condition may have associated eating issues you can check out the medical information on **Contact a Family**'s website: www.cafamily.org.uk, or call the helpline on: 0808 808 3555.

Allergy UK
www.allergyuk.org
01322 619898

Down's Syndrome Medical Interest Group
www.dsmig.org.uk

The **Health and Care Professionals Council** registers physiotherapists, occupational therapists, dieticians and speech and language therapists.
www.hpc-uk.org
0845 300 6184

Health and Care Professions Council, Park House, 184 Kennington Park Road, London, SE11 4BU

Health Visitors are registered with the Nursing and Midwifery Council
www.nmc-uk.org
020 7637 7181

University College, London's **Institute of Child Health**
www.ucl.ac.uk/ich/homepage
020 7242 9789
30 Guilford Street, London, WC1N 1EH

National Institute for Health and Clinical Excellence (NICE)
www.nice.org.uk
0845 003 7780
MidCity Place, 71 High Holborn, London, WC1V 6NA

Occupational therapists can be members of the **British Association of Occupational Therapists**
www.cot.co.uk
020 7357 6480

Physiotherapists can join the **Chartered Society of Physiotherapy**
www.csp.org.uk
020 7306 6666
14 Bedford Row, London, WC1R 4ED

Royal College of Psychiatrists
www.rcpsych.ac.uk
020 7235 2351
Belgrave Square, London, SW1X 8PG

Speech and Language Therapists can be found at the **Royal College of Speech and Language Therapists**
www.rcslt.org
020 7378 1200
RCSLT, 2 White Hart Yard, London, SE1 1NX

Experts consulted for this book

- Kate Barlow is a parent consultant at *www.parentconsultancy.com*.
- Teresa Bliss is an educational psychologist.
- Dr Gillian Harris BA, MSc, PhD is a senior lecturer and consultant clinical psychologist at the Children's Hospital, Birmingham.
- Melissa Hood is director of the Parent Practice; details of the organization can be found at www.theparentpractice.com.
- Penny Lazell runs www.healthvisitor4u.com, a private health visiting and children's sleep service. Penny is a registered general nurse and health visitor; she is also a qualified midwife and neonatal nurse.
- Sarah Newbury MRPharmS is a pharmacist.
- Charlotte Stirling-Reed is a registered public health nutritionist and an expert in paediatric nutrition. You can visit Charlotte's website at www.srnutrition.co.uk.
- Dr Pippa Rundle is a children's doctor and counsellor specializing in child and baby development issues and behavioural concerns. Get specialist information on Dr Pippa Rundle's work at www.drrundle.co.uk.
- Wendy Tomlinson is a life skills and law of attraction coach You can read more about Wendy's work by logging on to her site at www.wendytomlinsoncoaching.com/Parenting.
- Julia Wolman is a nutritionist specializing in baby and child nutrition and runs www.teenytummies.com.

Reading list

- Lauren Child, *I Will Not Ever Never Eat a Tomato* (Orchard, 2007)
- Antonia Chitty and Victoria Dawson, *Special Educational Needs: A Parent's Guide* (Need2Know Books, 2011)
- Antonia Chitty and Victoria Dawson, *Down's Syndrome: The Essential Guide* (Need2Know Books, 2010)
- George McClements, *Night of the Veggie Monster* (Bloomsbury, 2008)

Index